ACCIDENTAL
REVOLUTION

ACCIDENTAL REVOLUTION

THE STORY OF GRUNGE

—

KYLE ANDERSON

ST MARTIN'S GRIFFIN
NEW YORK

www.stmartins.com

Book design by Jonathan Bennett

Library of Congress Cataloging-in-Publication Data

Anderson, Kyle, 1982–
    Accidental revolution : the story of grunge / Kyle Anderson.–1st ed.
        p.   cm.
    ISBN-13: 978-0-312-35819-8
    ISBN-10: 0-312-35819-9
    1. Alternative rock music–History and criticism.   1. Title.

ML3534.A49   2007
781.66–dc22

                                                                2007010146

First Edition: July 2007

10 9 8 7 6 5 4 3 2 1

FOR LAUREN,

FINALLY

CONTENTS

ACCIDENTAL

REVOLUTION

—

INTRODUCTION

Just What the Hell Is This Stuff, Anyway?

ROCK IS DEAD, AND IT'S ALL AXL ROSE'S FAULT.

In 1991, Axl gathered together the latest incarnation of Guns N' Roses to begin the creation of what was to be their finest hour: *Use Your Illusion.* The songs that the Gunners were going to record were to be grandiose, epic, and unlike anything anybody had ever heard. Axl had already mapped out the interlinking videos that would be made in association with the album's multiple singles, and a massive stadium tour would be their worldwide victory lap to soak up all the glory that would rightfully be showered upon them. After all, they had given the world the greatest pair of rock-and-roll albums ever created—surely they deserved to exploit the rich benefits of such an accomplishment.

To say the sessions did not go well is an understatement. In fact, they stalled almost immediately. Axl and virtuoso guitarist Slash could not find common ground on many of the musical decisions. Slash wanted their sound to remain gritty and raw, just like their breakthrough debut, *Appetite for Destruction.* Axl thought that was small-time. He wanted to think bigger, louder, and gaudier, just like his idol Freddie Mercury. Drummer Steven Adler had been

1

replaced earlier that year, and his successor, former Cult skinsman Matt Sorum, did not mesh well with the rest of the group. In an effort to flesh out the sound, Axl hired keyboardist Dizzy Reed, further complicating the sessions and adding another personality to an already dysfunctional family. The sessions stopped and started; the album itself was delayed almost a year. Stories began to filter out of the studio about band dissension and possible departures, and rumor has it that Geffen, Guns' label, insisted that the record become a double album simply because they were afraid that it was the last they were ever going to hear of the band (so far, they've pretty much been right). It seemed like *Use Your Illusion* would be the undoing of Guns N' Roses and the undoing of big-time rock and roll in America.

For the time being, that would be only 50 percent correct. *Use Your Illusion I and II* was finally released on September 21, 1991, and was met with the overwhelming fanfare one would expect for a group that was arguably the most important rock band in the world. The singles went worldwide and the videos were big, splashy hits, and the Gunners were all set to embark on their epic tour around the world. But the good times hit a snag, and as 1991 came to a close, people began coming to a realization that would spell disaster for Axl Rose and all the metalheads he represented.

Use Your Illusion sucked.

In fact, it sucked on a couple of different levels. First and foremost, it didn't "rock" in the way that big rock records (especially records of the metal era) were supposed to rock. All the punk energy that had made *Appetite for Destruction* the most refreshing, dangerous album of the 1980s had been sterilized into stately ballads and middle-of-the-road blues tunes. There were a couple of flashes of throwback brilliance, but while *Use Your Illusion I* opener "Right Next Door to Hell" is a badass tune, it couldn't sniff the supercool jockstrap of "Welcome to the Jungle."

More important, *Use Your Illusion I and II* sucked on a grander scale in the sense that it was recorded proof that Axl Rose no longer meant anything to anybody except Axl Rose. On *Appetite for Destruction* (and *especially* on the *G N' R Lies* EP), Rose spoke for most of his fans: the small-town boy from the Midwest who was conflicted, confused, overwhelmed, excitable, and ambitious. The 1991 version of Axl was paranoid, self-serving, solipsistic, delusional, and probably more than a little bit deranged. Theoretically, Axl should have been at his angriest, and in a way, he was—in the blustery epic "Get in the Ring," Axl whaled on rock journalists and went as far as calling out several of them *by name*. But the rest of the lyrics were based on an interior logic that could only be decoded if your name was Axl Rose, and while there's nothing wrong with rock lyrics that don't make any sense, you had better provide some big-honking riffs to back up the absurdity of the words (Iron Maiden has made quite a long career out of this concept). Of course, it's hard to hold a candle in the cold November rain. Now why were people supposed to care?

The realization was a slow process—initially, *Use Your Illusion* sold like gangbusters. Though the albums were sold separately, retailers reported that people were rarely buying the two volumes independently. Both discs went platinum shortly after they were released, mostly on the strength of very popular singles and videos such as "Don't Cry" and "November Rain." The Gunners were poised to take that victory lap around the world, and despite the fact that the band (and more specifically Axl) could never be called reliable when it came to doing things as basic as showing up for tour dates, anticipation was high. As the tour plans were in motion, though, someone did something to Axl Rose that nobody had ever done before (or at least gotten away with).

The person was Kurt Cobain. And he had the gall—the audacity!—to say no to Axl Rose, the reigning Coolest Motherfucker on the Planet.

Axl had been a big fan of Nirvana (he was often spotted wearing a Nirvana cap during the long lead-up to *Use Your Illusion*). This may have been a machination of David Geffen (who had both acts under his watch, though on different labels), but it made sense that Rose would be drawn to *Nevermind*'s punk attitude, huge guitars, and soft-then-loud dynamics. Since Nirvana was initially embraced by the mainstream as a metal band (though he wore a dress, Kurt still *appeared* on *Headbanger's Ball*), the Guns audience would have been onboard with an opening spot by Seattle's finest, especially if they received an endorsement from Rose. But when the Guns camp approached Cobain about the slot, Cobain said no. He didn't just talk the talk—he was honestly and truly offended by metal's (and specifically Rose's) misogyny and love of excess. Metallica ended up touring with the Gunners, and the tour was a disaster, with missed dates, subpar shows, and at least one legendary riot in Montreal, where Metallica front man James Hetfield was burned alive by his own pyro and, not wanting to be upstaged in the stupidity department, Axl walked off the stage three songs into his band's set. Canadians are a remarkably patient people, but even they won't put up with that level of bullshit.

Meanwhile, as the tour for *Use Your Illusion* was imploding, that album that Axl Rose probably loved (but now publicly hated based on principle) was climbing up the charts on the strength of the airplay and video for "Smells Like Teen Spirit." *Nevermind* became the number-one album in the country, and the last gasps of Axl and company were pathetic versions of the righteous noise they were used to producing. Axl's dreams of a *Use Your Illusion* video trilogy (featuring the videos for "Don't Cry," "November Rain," and "Estranged") fizzled in a sea of apathy and incoherence. Kids may be fickle, but they can spot desperation—they took one look at Axl, sitting on a seafloor with his arms wrapped around a dolphin (an unintentionally hilarious moment toward the end of the "Estranged" video) and realized that he was clutching at straws. Besides, their new savior was in a much cooler water-influenced video inviting them to come as they were.

The success of *Nevermind* opened the floodgates for dozens of bands who broke through to the mainstream without sacrificing their dignity or integrity in the process. Pearl Jam succeeded with their self-conscious seventies rock; Soundgarden turned Sabbath-style metal inside out; Alice in Chains channeled their confessional lyrics through the psych-rock prism of Iron Butterfly. It was a good time to be a fan of guitar music, because no matter what sort of guitar music you were into, there was *somebody* playing it with more passion and conviction than anybody had heard in a long time.

But much like Guns N' Roses, Nirvana burned out before they really had the chance to realize their potential. Both bands released watershed breakout albums followed by controversial sophomore efforts, and neither group existed for very long afterward. For Axl, the burnout clearly happened at some point during the creation of *Use Your Illusion* and the potential that was established by *Appetite for Destruction* went mostly wasted. When Cobain died, the concept of "alternative rock" was still fairly new, as far as the mainstream was concerned. Knock-off bands such as Candlebox and Stone Temple Pilots, who had little connection to the scene but still aped the Seattle sound in a bid for big bucks, were already clogging the airwaves, and after Kurt's death they stormed the barricades. Without Cobain, there was no one around to declare them lame, and so we had to deal with Silverchair. As quickly as the door was opened, it was shotgun-blasted shut.

An entire generation of young musicians was growing up with the sort of stuff that trickled onto the radio after Kurt's death, and it didn't take them long to figure out what was working and what wasn't. They copied Pearl Jam, which is not necessarily a bad idea, but they noticed that the artier stuff didn't sell as well as the heavy arena anthems of their first album. They copied Soundgarden, a fine pursuit on its own, but failed to take into account the intricacies of that band's songs. These young musicians went on to form bands such as Creed and Nickelback, and listeners were stuck with a whole generation of flaccid wannabes carrying the torch for mediocrity. They sold millions but were as empty as the hair-metal bands their forefathers had fought so hard to vanquish.

Nevermind is remembered as the album that saved rock and roll from the clutches of evil, but in reality, it ruined rock music for at least a generation. Everybody, from record executives, to journalists, to fans, is constantly on the lookout for the "next Nirvana." But unfortunately, a band like that cannot be found; it just has to *happen.* There can never be another band that will have both critical and commercial success while also ushering in other bands under a singular aesthetic for a complete and total revolution. They look for Soundgarden, but they settle for Godsmack.

But *Nevermind* would not have mattered as much had Axl not let everybody down with the *Use Your Illusion* debacle. Time has been kinder to *Use Your Illusion* (when taken in the context of Axl's breakdown and all of the weirdness since, it's a pretty compelling listen), but at the time it represented the end of what was already a fading era, and it gave way to rock and roll's last gasp: grunge.

The grunge era is a remarkably short one. It began with the Melvins and the Wipers brewing up a squalor in small Seattle clubs in the mideighties, and by the time Kurt took his own life in '94, the scene was essentially done. In pop music terms, a decade can be several lifetimes, but on a larger evolutionary scale, it is merely a blip on a radar screen. The grunge era was the last time rock music mattered, and whether they knew it or not, the angry, screaming unwashed masses from Seattle (and beyond) certainly made it good.

Though there were plenty of anticommercial elements in the music, grunge was still a part of pop culture, and evaluating pop culture is always tricky. Since rock music is meant to be about being young and cool and out of control, there is a disposable quality to even the most beloved or influential songs or bands. It's nearly impossible to judge anything based on the quality of the music, because most of the stuff coming out of any one scene or movement sounds pretty terrible outside of its original context. This is why disco is such a difficult thing to defend, as most of those songs sound absolutely insipid (unless you're coked out of your mind at Studio 54 wearing a sequined leisure suit, in which case everything sounds utterly earth-shattering). Grunge has the same problem. Though nobody was writing songs about *Beverly Hills 90210* or the first Bush administration, there is something that is undeniably nineties about grunge, and the sad fact is that much of the music has aged quite poorly. That's not necessarily a knock on the songs themselves, as no scene's music tends to hold up over time. There are only a handful of bands that manage to survive the razor's edge of history—it's a simple form of natural selection that helps to weed out the stuff that probably wasn't very good anyway.

So if judging based on the music is unfair, how can anybody put the grunge scene in a historical context and judge its merits? It has to be based on a series of criteria that may seem esoteric but is generally important. Right now, bands, albums, movies, and cultural phenomena from the grunge era can be viewed through the prism of history and it's still possible to evaluate the real-time influence of those things as well. For example, there are plenty of rock fans who still vividly remember the release of Pearl Jam's *Ten*. There is an entire generation of rock fans who snuck down into the living room after their parents had gone to sleep so they could watch *120 Minutes* and see the video for "Alive." Those same fans might have followed Pearl Jam throughout their entire career, or they might have moved on to other bands or genres but still observed the Pearl Jam story arc from a distance. In the present day, the images and songs that have lasted are the ones that have somehow avoided the crushing blow of natural selection: Eddie Vedder falling from a balcony in the "Alive" video, the clip for "Jeremy," the performance of "Rockin' in the Free World" with Neil Young at the MTV Video Music Awards. A number of other associations also pop up in the Pearl Jam pantheon, like Ticketmaster, bootlegs, and "Last Kiss."

What is important to remember is that these things are not a career—a career is made up of hundreds of live shows and a dozen studio albums and interviews and videos and business decisions. But the scope of pop culture has a narrowing effect—the more time elapses, less and less is visible from the present. So cultural movements are boiled down to a few key moments or references, and the rest is cut away. There may be legions of people who were attached to the song "Why Go" (from *Ten*), but Pearl Jam will not be remembered for "Why Go"—it simply doesn't resonate over time. Hardcore fans may bristle at such a reductionist idea, but it's the way of the world when dealing with pop music, and it even happens to the best of bands. On a macrolevel, nobody will ever remember the length and breadth of Led Zeppelin's career, but they will remember "Whole Lotta Love," "Stairway to Heaven," and the death of John Bonham. "Serious" fans might remember "Living Loving Maid" (and there's no harm in that, considering it's a great song), but history will not. This attitude doesn't just work against great bands, but it also helps to diminutize terrible bands. Though they both had long careers filled with varied musical experiments and nongrunge developments, Stone Temple Pilots and Bush will both be remembered mostly as wannabes, though their front men will be remembered as a guy who took a lot of drugs and Gwen Stefani's husband, respectively. Natural selection is a cruel mistress, but it's often right.

But now that the grunge era is comfortably in the past and the fallout is finally being absorbed and processed, what is that scene's true place in the pantheon of rock? When future civilizations comb through the wreckage of our society thousands of years from now, how will they treat these noisy, angsty songs that for one brief shining moment made a group of unlikely musicians the de facto kings (and queens) of the world? This book will attempt to find a proper context for those years and ask the questions that have never been asked before (or at least never all at once): How did Kurt Cobain manage to reseed and obliterate the rock landscape with the same set of actions and circumstances? How did Pearl Jam contribute to the rise of Fred Durst? And what the hell does Axl Rose have to do with all of this?

Son (don't call me Daughter), have I got a little story for you. . . .

CHAPTER 1

—

THE EARLY YEARS

The Primordial Ooze Takes Shape

MOST OF AMERICA HAD NO IDEA WHAT GRUNGE WAS UNTIL 1991, when they saw a shabby-looking dude from Aberdeen, Washington, screaming at them about "a denial." But grunge actually started a decade prior to the release of "Smells Like Teen Spirit." It didn't have a name yet and it was still finding its legs, but the first glimpse of what was to come spent most of the 1980s staying safely below the surface and in the dark fringe clubs in the city of Seattle.

Like the rest of the Pacific Northwest, Seattle is an extremely strange corner of the universe. Just about every cliché, rumor, and urban legend about the greater Seattle area is true or just about true: It rains over three hundred days a year. There are a lot of old hippies. There are historically more serial killers per capita there than in any other area of the country. Even at their best, the Mariners will always be just slightly overrated. Though there had never been a musical movement that identified itself directly with the city, there are always way more bands than anybody has known what to do with. The joke around town is that it's rainy and depressing all the time, so obviously people are going to stay in their basements and play loud rock music, and that's really not too far from the truth. The "Seattle sound" is a wonderfully literal descriptor, as the music produced under that header *literally sounds like the city*: loud, slightly dirty, and somewhat depressing. Somehow, it even sounds *wet*–just think about the way the bass lines of Mudhoney tunes sort of sound like gurgling, as though the amps have been submerged in a mud pit.

In the 1980s, the American indie underground was probably at its peak. The punk explosion of the late 1970s, which saw the Sex Pistols, the Clash, and the Ramones capture the imaginations of hundreds of thousands of restless kids, was being explored and processed through a second generation of bands that were touring in vans, sleeping on floors, and getting drunk with their fans in a sort of underground socialist society of rock. The American Hardcore movement gave bands such as the Dead Kennedys, Black Flag, T.S.O.L., and Minor Threat a grassroots popularity and inspired a whole series of fanzines, tributes, and soundalike bands.

It's important to remember that though grunge became a worldwide phenomenon, it was essentially a local sound that ended up sneaking out of Seattle. It's no wonder so many local minds were fried when grunge became pop music. Historically speaking, there hadn't been a scene or a sound so defined by a place since 1960s London, and even then it wasn't as pronounced.

The local feel of the sound ended up being a sticking point for a lot of musicians and fans in the city of Seattle, and it created a lot of problems later when the spotlight began to swing toward Washington State. The sound consisted of a group of bands that existed in various forms for a decade, and then suddenly they were well-known outside of the confines of the Crocodile Cafe and the Central. Once people started trying to define "the Seattle sound" from the outside, a natural protective mechanism crept in. Seattleites take a great deal of pride in their city and tend to be overly protective. When the record labels and fair-weather fans came calling, they got pissed. Consequently, a lot of bands and fans seemed maladjusted and jaded by the time the outside world was paying attention to Seattle. But it wasn't so much that they were protective of the music (though they most certainly were); the real thing they wanted to protect was their *place*. People get testy when their home feels threatened; when the masses came calling, it felt like an invasion.

Though grunge bands eventually sprouted up across the country (and around the world), the sound of grunge (and even the word "grunge") will forever be linked with Seattle. Speaking broadly, the music tends to be dark and chaotic; it's clear that most of the tunes in the grunge era were written while it was raining outside. Even when bands didn't come from Seattle, it still *sounded* like they did. So when people started talking about "the Seattle sound" in reference to bands that had nothing to do with the underground movement that had been built up over a decade, it was only natural that people got defensive. Grunge was protected and defended in ways that most rock movements are not. Of course the fans who got there first are always going to shun the Johnny-come-latelies, but grunge also had the element of place working for it. People will go to bat for rock bands, but they'll absolutely go down swinging for their homes.

This branch of the eighties indie movement took their cues from punk rock but added elements of metal and subtracted the punk speed and structure. When the Seattle scene exploded, they became the seminal bands in the movement. It was a profoundly weird transition that a lot of bands went through once grunge broke: One minute they were unknown (and possibly broken up), and the next minute they were a highly influential force. Nobody experienced that change like Buzz "King Buzzo" Osborne, and no other band better defined the early days of grunge than his group the Melvins.

The Melvins first started playing together when the band members were still in high school in suburban Washington. Osborne was a fan of the hardcore scene but had no use for the velocity of punk, so much of the Melvins catalog (especially the early recordings) consists of hardcore songs slowed way down. When the speed was turned down, a number of other influences crept into the mix, like Sabbath-style metal and an an almost psychedelic approach to seering noise. Early Melvins recordings sound a lot like what Mudhoney would become, so it's no surprise that original Melvins bassist, Matt Lukin, later joined Mudhoney.

The Melvins continued to develop their slow, heavy, sludgy sound throughout the early 1980s, and by 1986 they were considered one of Seattle's best bands. That same year saw the release of *Deep Six*, a compilation album put together by local Seattleites Chris Hanzsek and Tina Casale on their C/Z Records label. The album brought together six like-minded bands to showcase what was going on in the Seattle rock community. Though the album was a commercial disappointment at the time, *Deep Six* is now a vital document in the history of grunge, as it represents the first recordings of a handful of bands that would later become legendary and also establishes the overriding concepts and the subtle nuances of the grunge sound.

The Melvins contributed four songs to the *Deep Six* album. Since they had been playing together the longest, their songs sound the most developed (conversely, Soundgarden had only been together a year, and though they sound accomplished, their recordings are pretty primitive) and they also have the most abrasive sound by far. Though it must have sounded completely foreign to anybody hearing it in 1986, a retrospective look at it makes it seem altogether obvious. Considering the bands that came later and gained fame and fortune, the songs on *Deep Six* were totally and completely logical.

—

THE MELVINS never received much commercial success and their records may not stand up over time, but they will forever remain important because of their association with Kurt Cobain. Though they were making albums long before he dreamed of *Nevermind*, Cobain's rub will always help the Melvins in their historical standing. Though he loathed the word "grunge" and had little sonic relationship to a lot of the seminal Seattle bands, Cobain was the most important icon of the grunge era. He was the one who broke out first, he was the one fans felt the most passion for, he was the one who was the most controversial, and he even died a mysterious death. Though he might not have made the best records or represented the scene or the city of Seattle the best, he's still an icon, and the only true icon grunge ever produced.

Cobain was a big fan of the Melvins. He first came to know them because drummer Dale Crover lived in Cobain's hometown of Aberdeen, Washington, and the Melvins rehearsed in Crover's basement. Cobain used to haul equipment for the band and even auditioned to play guitar in the group, though his efforts came up short. Later Cobain ended up helping produce Melvins albums, and after original Nirvana drummer Chad Channing left the group, Crover filled in on drums for a short tour, then later introduced the band to Scream drummer Dave Grohl, who would join the band on the skins for the duration of their existence.

Though they were by far the most influential of the protogrunge bands, the Melvins were not alone on the *Deep Six* compilation. The album also featured contributions from Soundgarden, Green River, and Malfunkshun, all of whom would become much bigger bands (in different versions, of course). The comp was rounded out by two bands that are rarely mentioned among the all-time great grunge groups but maintained a level of influence nonetheless. They were the U-Men and Skin Yard.

The U-Men were formed in 1981 by drummer Charlie Ryan, guitarist Tom Price, and front man John Bigley (original bass player Robin Buchan was replaced by Jim Tillman, and it's his tones heard on *Deep Six*). The U-Men had recorded before the release of *Deep Six*, having put out a self-titled EP in 1984. It's hard to pinpoint the U-Men's influences, as they were by far the most chaotic sounding of all the early grunge groups, but there are traces of Sabbath-style metal, jagged minimalist punk, and the droning noise of Suicide. The U-Men were known mostly for their riotous live performances, which were often shut down by police for inciting violent and destructive behavior. When they broke up in 1988, it had to have been the most passive implosion of any band in history, as nobody even bothered to tell Price, who showed up at the band's empty practice space three times before finally figuring out the the rest of the group had decided to pack it in.

What is notable about the U-Men is that Price and Ryan both were part of a sort of supergroup side project called Catbutt, who, like the U-Men, were notorious for wreaking havoc—they were even dropped from Sub Pop Records because they destroyed a tour van supplied by the label. But the most notable aspect of Catbutt had nothing to do with their music or their reputation and had everything to do with their name. Catbutt is a ridiculous band name that cannot possibly sound anything but goofy, juvenile, and a little dirty. That brand of humor, however, was not uncommon among the early grunge groups.

It's strange to consider bands as heavy and self-important as Soundgarden or Pearl Jam giggling like schoolchildren at the thought of a feline's ass, but potty humor was a stock-in-trade in early Seattle. Mudhoney once insisted that one of their releases come out on limited-edition "poop brown" vinyl. The Melvins' 1989 album, *Ozma* (released on Boner Records), contained the songs "The Heaviness of My Load" and "Over the Under Excrement." So what's the deal with all the dookie talk?

Though none of the breakout bands dealt in any of that sort of juvenalia (there's nothing funny about Nirvana's "Territorial Pissings"), that sense of humor did highlight one thing that was very, very important: This first wave was not taking itself seriously. These bands were making music they loved and doing it the way they wanted to. Based on these lyrics, they didn't have any interest in becoming rock stars (Catbutt might actually be the only band name less commercial than Butthole Surfers, who ironically would have a fluke hit in the post-Cobain era with "Pepper"). Those kinds of decisions are active, and those bands chose to be anti-commercial. But the fact that a lot of these bands had actual followings is a testament to the anything-goes nature of underground rock in the late eighties and early nineties. Catbutt actually had *buzz*. It's no wonder that Nirvana became huge—if the goofy guys can get critical acclaim in Europe and move thousands of copies of their independent EPs, how far could the serious guys go?

THE SIXTH band included on *Deep Six* was Skin Yard (another band with a pretty terrible name). Though Matt Cameron was an original member (he played drums on Skin Yard's contributions on *Deep Six* before joining fellow *Deep Six*ers Soundgarden a year later), the most influential member of Skin Yard was guitarist Jack Endino, who later made a name for himself as a producer and recorded so many of the early grunge bands and contributed so profoundly to their sound that he eventually took on the mantle of

"The Godfather of Grunge." Skin Yard released five fairly nonde-script albums of relatively straightforward rock (they were easily the least edgy of all the bands on *Deep Six*) and provided a development ground for rockers such as Cameron, Jason Finn (later of the Presidents of the United States of America), and Barrett Martin (Screaming Trees, Mad Season), but their legacy will be all about Endino.

Jack Endino is a fascinating character; in a town and a scene full of interesting people, he might be the most colorful. He'll readily admit that he is a nerd for production and has a sort of easygoing, cavalier attitude that is probably why he has worked generally nonstop since his first production credits back in the eighties. Endino produced Nirvana's first full-length, *Bleach*, and also helped establish the sounds of Soundgarden, Mudhoney, and a bunch of other bands that held the same aesthetic. Interestingly, it might very well be Endino who was resposible for bringing the grunge sound together, as he found the common sonic threads between bands that were generally pretty disparate. Endino has always been good at making bands sound like what they sound like, but in the grunge era he managed to bring them together. For example, Kim Thayil and Mark Arm are wildly different guitar players, but the tones on *Screaming Life* and *Superfuzz Bigmuff* have more in common that is immediately recognizable. If Sub Pop was Motown Records, then Endino was their Ashford & Simpson.

It isn't just Endino's production style that sets him apart, though. Endino was always open to producing just about anybody (and he still is—on his official Web site, he addresses people who wish to get recorded by him with this statement: "If I like your demo, we'll talk"), which speaks to the larger anything-goes attitude that permeated the grunge landscape. Just look at the number of bands that contained members of other bands—it seemed as though no musician in Seattle ever said no to anything.

However, such an open sense of community is not always the path to utopia; in fact, it ultimately makes people take you less seriously. Considering the number of influential bands he produced and his participation in designing the grunge sound, Endino's production peers should be Rick Rubin, Bob Rock, and Mutt Lange. None of those guys ever invite submissions on their personal Web pages. The "everyone's invited" attitude is excellent for attracting new fans and helping the scene to grow, but from a historical perspective, it hurts the importance of individuals. Endino did produce Soundgarden and Nirvana, but he also produced bands such as Fluid, Coffin Break, and Seaweed. When everybody is allowed in, nobody seems special. The perception is not that you believe that everybody deserves a fair shot but that you can't tell the difference between a great band like Soundgarden and a mediocre band like Seaweed.

So when the Seattle scene suddenly broke out and everybody focused on the bands trying to cut the wheat from the chaff, the greater populace (who prior to 1991 had no interest in grunge) made the decisions about who was great and who wasn't. When it was decided that Nirvana was going to graduate to superstardom and Coffin Break would get left behind, it was shocking to find out that both of those bands had been produced by the same guy and that they were equally beloved within Seattle. An egalitarian spirit works well in a localized scene, but that sort of cultural socialism can't sustain itself on a national level, so when the local scene became *everybody's* scene, bands were excluded and the fates of those bands that were absorbed by the national media were taken out of the hands of the locals. This was a far more jarring thing than people may realize—when Nirvana and the rest went national, Seattle suffered from empty-nest syndrome. Though it sounds overdramatic, success really was the worst thing that happened to the Seattle bands, and it was never more difficult to be a fan once everybody broke out.

THERE WERE dozens more bands that weren't on *Deep Six* who contributed to the development of the Seattle sound, especially early Mark Arm bands Mr. Epp and the Calculations and the Limp Richerds. There were also plenty of groups outside of Seattle that contributed to the primordial ooze from which grunge emerged. One of those bands was the much-beloved Massachusetts group Dinosaur Jr. Fronted by guitar-playing weirdo J Mascis and his high school friend Lou Barlow, Dinosaur Jr. trafficked in incredibly loud, seriously sloppy, feedback-heavy punk rock with a major Neil Young fetish. Not nearly as dark as most of the Seattle acts, the band had a penchant for noise and knack for melody (something that most of the American indie underground kept under a blanket of fuzz) that made them a perfect complement to the Seattle sound. They were never directly associated with the grunge era, but their brush with crossover success in the early nineties (they had minor *120 Minutes* hits with "Out There" and "Feel the Pain") was likely due to the shine that came off of bands such as Nirvana and Soundgarden. Mascis's sloppy, almost jammy noise clearly rubbed off on Pearl Jam, and the combination of feedback and jubilation on Dinosaur's mideighties albums is a clear precursor to *In Utero*.

In a tradition that was later carried on by Smashing Pumpkins, there were a number of midwestern interlopers who also contributed to the grunge sound. Of all these, the Replacements were by far the most popular and influential. Based out of Minneapolis, the Replacements were the most talented pack of drunks in history. Fronted by Paul Westerberg, they played punk songs with a healthy dose of Americana that were then soaked in beer suds. Their middle-period albums *Tim* and *Pleased to Meet Me* are classics, representing some of the best music produced in the United States in the eighties. In fact, *Tim*, which was released around the same time as *Deep Six*, might be the most influential album of the pregrunge years on the bands that would later become international superstars.

The connection to Pearl Jam is fairly obvious, as *Tim* utilizes a lot of seventies rock tropes and incorporates some roots-rock stylings, all played as punk tunes. There is a lot of "Kiss Me on the Bus" in "State of Love and Trust." But Kurt Cobain was a fan of the Replacements, too. "Left of the Dial" has an about-to-fall-apart quality that makes it exciting and unstable the same way that "Lithium" sounds like it could break down at any minute. The Replacements also experimented with the quiet verse/loud chorus dynamics that became an alt-rock staple throughout most of the nineties (the Pixies, another of Cobain's favorite groups, mastered that art as well).

Westerberg's influence on grunge was later formally confirmed through his appearances on the sound track to the Cameron Crowe film *Singles*. Westerberg contributed two solo tunes to the actual sound track (his first recordings since the breakup of the Replacements), and also contributed music to the film's score. Westerberg has since evolved into a sort of grunge troubadour, releasing albums of solo acoustic songs that sound suspiciously like they could have been written in 1990.

But the band that might be the most important group to champion the cause of grunge and heavily contribute to its breakout is a band that people rarely consider when recalling the Seattle scene. That's logical, especially considering they were from Georgia, but there's no way that grunge happens without R.E.M.

R.E.M. was the first great American postpunk success story. Through word-of-mouth reviews, nonstop touring, and critical acclaim, R.E.M. went from being a college-town bar band to being a national sensation, gaining media attention as early as 1983, when *Rolling Stone* named their debut album, *Murmur*, the best of that year. Their rise throughout the eighties was slow and steady, culminating with their massive breakout one-two punch of *Out of Time* and *Automatic for the People*, the former of which was released in 1991, the same year that saw *Nevermind* and *Ten* hit the charts.

R.E.M. was the most successful American indie band because they managed to be everything to everyone. They had folk influences, they had power-pop elements, and they even got a little funky now and then. When you think about it, Pearl Jam is simply an extremely loud version of R.E.M. with some occasional Zeppelin guitar squiggles thrown in for good measure. More important, R.E.M.'s success proved that bands could make the crossover from their own insulated universe into the mainstream and still maintain their integrity and dignity, a concept that inspired and empowered plenty of esoteric bands looking to score big at the end of the millennium.

But if R.E.M. was so vital, why is it that the band almost *never* gets mentioned when people wax poetically about the great American rock nineties, when indies ruled the universe? Sonically, R.E.M. was of course much milder than, say, Soundgarden (their fuzzed-out, turned-to-11 masterpiece *Monster* didn't come out until 1994). Philosophically, however, R.E.M. would have been right in the pocket with the Seattleites, as they sang about loneliness, isolation, and yearning. They had a nontraditional front man with a distinct voice, and they had a strange nonsexuality to them, as though none of the band members had genitalia (which was similarly true of groups like Alice in Chains—did those guys even have an ounce of sexuality? That's probably why Layne Staley was able to wear a dress onstage and it seemed normal, because it was no more or less comfortable than the alternative).

Maybe R.E.M. simply remained separate from the grunge

bands because their success was sort of a foregone conclusion; *Automatic for the People* would have sold 5 million albums whether Pearl Jam had released *Vs.* or not. But the American South will not be denied, and R.E.M. is more important to the grunge era than anyone has ever acknowledged. They paved the way for the crossover. R.E.M. helped instill faith in the power (both aesthetic and economic) of a band that did it the way they wanted to do it.

THOUGH NONE of them caught even a whiff of the same commercial success their protégés would later collect, the early grunge bands helped establish not only a sonic quality that other bands toyed with and mutated over time but also an attitude and a general aesthetic that, for better or for worse, dictated what grunge was and what it would become in the next decade. *Deep Six* didn't move a lot of units, but it did embolden plenty of bands to come to the table, and that's how revolutions usually begin.

CHAPTER 2

—

GREEN RIVER

Metal Meets Punk, Then Challenges It to a Duel

THE YEAR 1985 WAS NOT A GOOD ONE TO BE IN SEATTLE, ESPE-
cially if you were a musician or a rock fan. In a move befitting John
Lithgow's puritan reverend in *Footloose* (a film coincidentally released the year before), the town council enacted the Teen Dance
Ordinance (TDO), which effectively destroyed a club's ability to
put on all-ages shows. This may not seem like a terrible liability,
but make no mistake: Though there may be plenty of twentysomethings drinking at your local rock club, those small venues
live and die by the all-ages crowds. Prior to the introduction of the
TDO, Seattle clubs were mostly unregulated, so they were able to
operate under their own rules and parameters. Once the TDO was
introduced, local venues suddenly had to hire more security to
keep a more watchful eye on their clientele, plus spend exorbitant
amounts of money on insurance policies that had become manda-
tory for operation. The effects were so far-reaching that several
clubs shut down completely, and by 1986 it had become so hard
to put on shows that a handful of bands decided to call it quits.

One of the bands that managed to survive was Green River. In
1985, the year clubs were shuttering their doors and bands were

packing it in, they released *Come On Down,* a six-track EP, on Homestead Records. Though bands like Malfunkshun and Soundgarden were arguably more popular among followers of the scene, Green River managed to be the first of those groups to put an album out; considering it beat the *Deep Six* compilation to the street by about six months, *Come On Down* can be considered the first grunge album.

As an introduction, it's rather unremarkable—its six songs feel like less-refined mash-ups of Mudhoney and eighties metal (which, in reality, is *exactly* how it's supposed to sound). It did manage to set a few precedents that were important to the development of grunge, though.

The first thing that jumps out immediately is the production. As a word, "grunge" makes the most sense as an adjective. On *Come On Down* everything sounded "dirty," sure, but there was also a certain thickness that was taken from early Black Sabbath albums. This was almost certainly intentional—most bands (Soundgarden especially) were clearly Sabbath disciples—but there was a line of practical reasoning for sounding filthy as well. The first should be relatively obvious: It's cheap. Getting records to sound clean is expensive and time-consuming, but recording on an eight-track and turning everything up extremely loud is quick, easy, and doesn't break the bank. Clearly the sound was established long before anybody had any sort of rock stardom or credibility, so putting out cheap albums was a necessity. This isn't unique to the grunge movement—unless you're Coldplay or some other group constructed solely on the prettiness of your sound, most early work sounds cheap.

Of course, nothing is done solely for practical reasons, and there were constructed motives behind grunge bands sounding like they did. The most dismissive assertion is that grunge bands played sloppy, down-tuned songs because they couldn't actually play their instruments, write songs, or perform. This is a common argument about punk rock, except that anti–punk rockers accuse punks of using speed to mask their lack of musicianship. That argument doesn't really hold water for grunge, though, especially considering the musical pedigrees of many of the musicians involved. Most bands made the noise they made to try to get noticed, but not in the traditional way.

In the mideighties, the sound of the moment was metal (sometimes referred to as "glitter rock," "hair metal," or, if you lived in the Pacific Northwest, "horseshit"), so that was the music that underground bands were supposed to hate but secretly aspired to be like. Metal was not necessarily a regional phenomenon (in fact, no other genre has arguably been as "global" as metal), but it did have a symbolic hometown in Los Angeles. Mötley Crüe, Guns N' Roses, and Poison all called Los Angeles home, and since it was by far the most decadent city in America in the 1980s, it made sense as both a spiritual home and an inspiration for the coke-and-whore-laden tunes of Reagan America. It's been well documented that a lot of bands in the grunge idiom aspired to be metalheads earlier in their tenure: Andrew Wood came across as a very metalesque front man; Alice in Chains was called Alice N Chainz and was signed as a metal act; Soundgarden had long hair and played Sabbath riffs. The point is this: There were clearly metal sympathizers among the grunge elite. So why would they actively attempt to torpedo those bands once success came calling?

The answer is somewhat subversive. The flight from LAX to SEATAC is barely three hours in length, but the distance might as well be measured in millennia. Any sort of "West Coast scene" was lucky if it got as far as San Francisco; as far as California was concerned, the state of Washington was simply an ugly hat. Today it's odd to think about Seattle as anything but a hub for rock music, considering the success of grunge and the subsequent breakouts of

Seattle bands such as Death Cab for Cutie, but prior to 1991 the city was simply a secondary tour stop for national groups. For bands based in the city, not only was going national an impossibility, but establishing any sort of regional presence was also difficult. Several bands attempted to make waves in Los Angeles, and some even had a bit of success (Soundgarden, most notably), but for all intents and purposes, Seattle was simply a rock-and-roll stepchild.

Even though the bands knew that metal was the pathway to groupies and (better) drugs, they subconsciously knew that particular quest for fire was a total uphill battle, which is why *Come On Down* (and most of the other early grunge records) is the sound of hair metal being mocked. Green River guitarist and Mudhoney front man Mark Arm would probably contend that they were simply trying to make as much noise as possible, but the model for early grunge albums involved taking a metal riff and ruining its life by playing it backward, distorting it, burying it in feedback, slowing it down, breaking equipment, and shouting a-melodic lyrics on top of it. It wasn't until after the national spotlight found the Seattle scene that the bands realized that the best way to sound cool was to openly mock the already fading dinosaurs of the metal era. Grunge bands had been mocking them for years on record, but it had been subversive, sonic mockery; they didn't realize it could be lucrative until much later.

IN 1982, University of Washington student Mark McLaughlin put out a seven-inch EP titled *Of Course I'm Happy, Why?* with his band Mr. Epp, a group he had put together when he was still in high school (when the band was called Mr. Epp and the Calculations, a tribute to a math teacher at Bellevue Christian High School, which three of the band members attended). A punk band in the T.S.O.L./Minor Threat tradition, Mr. Epp actually generated quite a bit of underground buzz in the early eighties. McLaughlin (who had taken on the punk-rock moniker Mark Arm, which he has stuck with ever since) published a fanzine called *The Attack* that gained the attention of Sonic Youth and the Butthole Surfers (both of which were already established in the national indie underground). Mr. Epp even had a song called "Mohawk Man" that gained some notoriety in the nefarious premetal L.A. market when it became the number-one song on KROQ's *Rodney on the Rocks*, hosted by Rodney Bingenheimer. The song unseated, of all things, Toni Basil's "Mickey," which was a national number-one hit. The band played shows locally and opened for more national acts such as the Dead Kennedys and even opened a show for Nina Hagen in front of an understandably hostile crowd. While rock stardom was an impossibility (especially in new-wave- and metal-gorged 1983), the band still generated something of a following.

One of their fans was a guitarist named Steve Turner, whom Arm had met at local punk shows and who ended up joining Mr. Epp in 1983. Like Arm, Turner discovered punk rock when he was in high school and was slowly working his way back to garage rock and the fuzzed-out chaos of the Stooges. Because of his like-mindedness with Arm, Turner fit right in with the Mr. Epp aesthetic. Unfortunately, the synergy in that particular context was short-lived, as Mr. Epp broke up in February of 1984. Their farewell show was emblematic of their approach to music and their sense of humor: Opening for Malfunkshun, they closed their set with a thirty-minute version of their song "Flogging" that culminated in a series of smoke bombs going off and a giant bagful of hair being dumped on the audience.

Despite their relative notoriety, the breakup of Mr. Epp did not send shock waves through the Seattle music community. Still, the locals had become aware of Arm and were curious what his next move would be. He and Turner decided they needed to form a new band, so Turner recruited his old high school friend Stone Gossard, who had played with Turner in a band called the Ducky Boys. All three men were friendly with a bass player named Jeff Ament, who played in a few different groups but spent most of his time in an outfit called Deranged Diction. Initially, Ament resisted joining the band (he had seen Mr. Epp several times and hated them), but Arm and Turner were persistent and eventually convinced him to enter the fold. Arm got another friend of his, Alex Vincent, to play drums. The new band decided to call themselves Green River as an homage to the Green River Killer, who murdered almost fifty women in the Pacific Northwest in the early eighties. Because of the overabundance of guitarists in the band, Arm left his axe behind and assumed vocal duties.

Green River's first show was on July 1, 1984, opening for a band called Positive Metal Attitude. The band made an impression and was soon invited to play more gigs, opening for touring acts such as the Dead Kennedys, the Melvins, and Malfunkshun. Once, at the Gorilla Gardens, Green River opened for Sonic Youth. Thurston Moore was so impressed by them that he requested Green River as Sonic Youth's official opening act every time they played Seattle.

By December of 1984, the band was ready to record an album. The six songs they put down became *Come On Down*, which was released in 1985 on the local Homestead label. As discussed earlier, it's metal as played by the Stooges, and the strange pull between the punk and metal worlds was all too intriguing for rock fans, so *Come On Down* gained a following and Green River ostensibly became the first grunge band.

Unhappy with the band's metal leanings even despite Arm's strong influence, Steve Turner left the band shortly after the completion of *Come On Down*. He shifted his focus to his side project, a ridiculous little noise band called the Thrown Ups. Though Arm could have easily filled in on guitar, Jeff Ament recruited his friend and fellow Deranged Diction bandmate Bruce Fairweather to play the six-string. Green River, Version 2.0, was ready to take the next step.

With the TDO in full effect and *Come On Down* and the *Deep Six* compilation both in the can, Green River decided to hit the road and head east in the fall of 1985. They opened several shows for Big Black, then broke off to do their own shows in New Jersey and New York, where they played their first-ever show at the legendary punk venue CBGB. Unfortunately, *Come On Down* was not yet available in New York, so their show at CBGB was supposedly only attended by six people (two employees and four Japanese tourists, so the story goes). Following another disastrous show in Detroit opening for the Glenn Danzig–led goth punkers Samhain, Green River returned to Seattle for something of a residence at the Ditto Tavern.

Unease was already beginning to develop within the band. Arm, now without the support of the like-minded Turner, was starting to become overwhelmed not only by the metal leanings of his bandmates but also by the blatant careerism they often exhibited. Arm wanted the band to be successful, but he wanted it to happen organically; meanwhile, Ament was courting A&R representatives from major labels. Ament's active courtship of a record deal was not very punk rock, and Arm sometimes took it personally.

Musically, Arm was also on the defensive about many aspects of how the group's sound was developing, and you can hear the tension building on their follow-up to *Come On Down*. The five-track EP, titled *Dry as a Bone*, was recorded in its entirety in June of 1986. Dissatisfied with the perceived lack of commitment at Homestead, Green River opted to put their next release out on a local label started by Bruce Pavitt, called Sub Pop. It took Pavitt nearly a year to get the money together to actually release the album in 1987, so

Green River continued to play shows around town at the same three or four clubs, since many venues had either given up on trying to put on rock shows under the tyranny of the TDO or shuttered their doors entirely. The bands that appeared on the *Deep Six* compilation (Soundgarden, the Melvins, Malfunkshun, Skin Yard, and the U-Men, along with Green River) would all share bills or go to one another's shows, so the feeling of an actual scene started to develop. In fact, by the end of 1986, Seattle rock writer and scenester Jonathan Poneman (who would later join up with Bruce Pavitt to run Sub Pop and sign Nirvana) made a prediction in a column in the local altweekly *The Rocket*: "The town right now is in a musical state where there is an acknowledgement of a certain consciousness." He concluded by simply saying, "Something's gonna happen."

DRY AS A BONE was released on Sub Pop in July of 1987. As an album, it is both a logical extension of *Come On Down* and yet something of a departure. Their previous release struck an interesting balance between punk and metal, but without the influence of Turner, Arm was the lone punk among a group of metal guys, so while the pace of *Dry as a Bone* is still very punk influenced, the guitars are very clean and the riffs owe more to seventies rock than anything else. It still feels like grunge, though, mostly because of Arm's unique yelping vocals, which would later be put to their best use on Mudhoney classics such as "Touch Me I'm Sick." *Dry as a Bone* was one of the first albums produced by Jack Endino, a guitarist in Skin Yard who later went on to produce many of the cornerstone albums in the Seattle scene, like Nirvana's *Bleach* and Mudhoney's *Superfuzz Bigmuff*. One sonic element that *Dry as a Bone* did establish that runs through the entire grunge oeuvre is the sound of the drums—they are absolutely arena size in a way that

wasn't evident on *Come On Down.* Perhaps the most notable foot-
note about *Dry as a Bone* is its listing in a Sub Pop catalog, written
by Bruce Pavitt. In the write-up, Pavitt refers to *Dry as a Bone* as
"ultra-loose grunge," and while the term "grunge" had been used
to describe bands as far back as the 1960s, it was the first time the
word had ever been formally associated with a group in the Seattle
scene.

Though there was dissent among the ranks, the band was still
known as one of the tightest outfits in the entire scene, and they became known for their somewhat mischievous onstage demeanor.
Late in 1986, Green River played at the Paramount Ballroom in
Seattle, opening a show for Public Image Ltd., the band fronted by
former Sex Pistol Johnny Rotten. After a blistering set, Mark Arm
closed the proceedings by telling the crowd to "stick around if you
want to see what a real sellout looks like." The crowd, won over by
their local boys, heckled Rotten relentlessly during his set (though
that was reportedly a common reaction during that particular PIL
tour). While he was performing, the band stole a chair that Rotten
had brought with him, and Andrew Wood, the Malfunkshun front
man who was also friends with the band, took all of Rotten's wine
that was provided to him backstage.

At another show in 1987 at the Central Tavern in Seattle, the
crowd decided to start throwing Spam at Green River in the middle
of their set. The band, not wanting to be one-upped by the crowd,
dropped their instruments and threw the meat product right back.
Not only did this get Green River banned for life from the venue,
but it also started a trend for them: The band gained a reputation
for throwing some sort of food product at their audience (cooking
oil was a popular choice).

In August of 1987, Green River went back into the studio to
record an eight-track full-length titled *Rehab Doll.* Though Jack
Endino produced several preproduction tracks, the knob-twiddling

duties ended up falling to Bruce Calder, who would later produce Mother Love Bone. That is telling–though Green River splintered off into Mudhoney and Mother Love Bone, *Rehab Doll* sounds like demos for the latter. The most notorious nod to that development is the rerecording of "Swallow My Pride," which originally appeared on *Come On Down*. The new version was significantly cleaner and sharper and even featured melodic backing vocals that offset Arm's voice. The lead vocals were another issue–Arm was reined in a great deal, and it shows. The abandon he had shown on *Dry as a Bone* was nowhere to be found on *Rehab Doll*, significantly shifting the sound into a much more metal-influenced and populist direction.

Arm's voice was a big bone of contention in the band. Ament, aware that the band was clicking on all cylinders and could sign a major-label deal at any time, was encouraging Arm to get singing lessons, a suggestion he wholeheartedly opposed. The professional rift between Ament and Arm finally came to a head at a big show in October of 1987, which would end up being the last show Green River would ever play.

The band had been invited to Los Angeles to open for Jane's Addiction. Jane's self-titled debut had already made waves among the industry, and the band was in the midst of a huge major-label bidding war. They would later sign with Warner Bros., who then put out the now-classic *Nothing's Shocking* in 1988. Green River saw this as an opportunity to get noticed by the industry, so Ament earmarked a handful of backstage passes for various A&R representatives around Los Angeles. When Arm found out, he was crushed; he had wanted some of his friends to take those passes so they could see his band play for free. It didn't help matters that few of the passes actually got used, as most of the invitees didn't appear for the show.

Though they played a blistering forty-minute set, the show in Los Angeles signified the end of Green River. The band formally broke up on Halloween 1987; by the time *Rehab Doll* was released in June of 1988, everyone in Green River was already in a new band (save for Alex Vincent, who moved to Japan and became a lawyer). Gossard, Ament, and Fairweather formed the Lords of the Wasteland (later christened Mother Love Bone once Malfunkshun front man Andrew Wood joined the fold), and Arm hooked up with his old friend Steve Turner to form Mudhoney. Green River was no more.

Interestingly, the breakup of Green River stemmed entirely from professional animosity; unlike normal band breakups, nobody seemed to take anything personally. Later, when Ament and Gossard formed Pearl Jam, they went on the road with Turner and Arm's Mudhoney all the time. Often the two bands would get together for encores to play Green River songs, which turned into minor reunion events (minus Vincent, of course). The friendliness continues to this day: Arm says he and Jeff Ament still skateboard together all the time, despite their past creative differences (and the fact that they're both in their forties).

IN THE annals of rock history, Green River is usually earmarked not so much for what it did but for what it led to. Since it laid the seeds for both Pearl Jam and Mudhoney, Green River probably would have been considered "important" even if they were terrible or had never released any music. But Green River was more than just a developing ground for musicians who would go on to greater things; in fact, it set several precedents that carried through grunge's rise to ubiquity and its fall from grace. The most obvious of these precedents was the sound—the sludge of metal on the low end combined with the maniacism of punk on top was essentially the formula that Nirvana grew into by the height of their career.

Green River's lyrical influence should also not be underestimated. The bulk of their songs weren't about girls or rebellion, the typical rock-and-roll mainstays. Rather, Green River songs were mostly existentialist nightmares about isolation and suffering—one of their most famous songs, "Ain't Nothing to Do," is *literally* about being bored. Such navel-gazing would become a staple of the grunge era, both musically and socially—existential angst, coupled with self-loathing and irony, became the talking points for an entire generation.

Even Green River's breakup became emblematic of the times. Rather than have blowouts, bands simply faded into the ether without much animosity, and the band members typically remained friends, if not collaborators. Of course, this could be emblematic of the general disposition of the city of Seattle—it has to be one of the most unemotional cities in the country (it's no wonder irony found a home here). But even with that in mind, Mark Arm's relationship with Jeff Ament is pretty amazing and should not be taken lightly. Green River's personnel all became more famous in arguably better bands, but their short reign as Seattle's most popular act established a cultural foundation that would affect life as we knew it for a solid decade. Even though there were inklings that something was bound to happen sooner or later, Arm, Ament, and the rest couldn't have possibly known what was about to go down.

In fact, the breakup of Green River might have been the most important cultural milestone in grunge's sordid history, even though we can only really appreciate it retroactively. When bands break up, any mention of "artistic differences" is usually code for "the singer slept with the drummer's wife" or "the singer is skimming money off the top" or "the drummer keeps trying to sleep with the singer" (this final example only applies to Fleetwood Mac). "Artistic differences" is more or less a rock-and-roll cliché, used to mask petty arguments with supposed grandiose disagreements about influences, sound, and the direction of a band.

However, in Green River's case, you couldn't define their separation as anything but "artistic differences." The band was composed of viewpoints from two relative extremes, and those extremes could no longer coexist. However, their ability to transcend a cliché does not make them impressive; rather, it's what their end represented that made it definitive. Unwittingly, their disagreement over the direction of a marginal band led to the end of rock and roll.

Arm's ideals (along with those of future Mudhoney partner Steve Turner) were firmly rooted in anticommercialism. As Mr. Epp had proven and Mudhoney would later drive home, Arm had no use for hooks, melody, or even tuning—he was interested in visceral noise and cacophony, delivered with ragged force. In rock music, there is an accepted altruism to following this sort of path. The belief is that anything that is consciously anticommercial is inherently better than a similar sort of music played with careerist intentions. This makes perfect sense—rock music appeals mostly to young people, and most young people want to believe that they are both antiestablishment and wholly independent in their idealism. In the very specific reality of high school study halls in 1990, Mudhoney was Led Zeppelin.

As far as the construction of the public persona for most bands in the grunge movement went, they were the righteous warriors saving music fans from the artificiality of metal. The argument was turned into a black-and-white "you're-either-with-us-or-against-us" scenario. You either stood for the empty, decadent overlords (metal) or the message-driven, wholesome working class (grunge). Naturally, such a gross overgeneralization can never be accurate, and the average fan didn't define it that way. Most Nirvana fans probably still spun their Guns N' Roses discs well after the former band made the latter irrelevant.

This is not to say that grunge bands put out more accessible albums than metal bands. In reality, early grunge was almost entirely inaccessible because (1) the albums were dissonant and grating and (2) they were not easily found in stores (thus covering both definitions of the word "accessible" in this context). The real accessibility came from the forwardness of the bands and their members, or at least the perception of this phenomenon. Early Mudhoney, for example, made music that was dissonant and difficult, and they made it right in front of the listener. The mistakes were right up there in the mix; sometimes, the mistakes were the focus. It's no wonder that notoriously difficult producer Steve Albini saw his greatest spike in popularity during this era, as his recording style highlights the natural mistakes and imperfections of a band playing in a room together. Most rock stars create a sort of "role model of cool" for those around them (what kid in 1987 *didn't* want to be Axl or Vince or Sebastian?), but the figureheads of the grunge era didn't want anybody to have to live up to their level; if anything, they wanted to step down to their audience's level.

This sort of attitude had a devastating effect on rock music for a handful of years. Suddenly it was totally unacceptable for a rock star to actually act like a rock star. If you didn't stand for something greater and acted on any level other than that of common fans, you were cast out as a traitor to everything that rock and roll stood for (or something like that). This is why people were so offended by Scott Weiland back when Stone Temple Pilots debuted. It's true that their debut single seemed way too derivative of Pearl Jam, but the thing that offended the rock elite was that Weiland sang (typically without a shirt) about sex, power, and decadence. He seemed to do drugs not because he had been abused and needed an escape but because he liked getting high. He made the cardinal rock-star mistake of 1994—he had fun.

Green River's legacy as a "transitional" band sometimes seems unfair but is mostly accurate. They put out a handful of good songs, made their mark touring, and make for an excellent slice of rock trivia. But their defining moment was their breakup, which was one of the best breakups in history, as it allowed everybody to join better bands that would make the most influential music at the end of the millennium.

CHAPTER 3

—

MOTHER LOVE BONE

Big Songs, Big Boas, Big Tragedy

ELVIS AARON PRESLEY WAS BORN ON JANUARY 8, 1935, IN A TINY town in Mississippi called Tupelo. Love him or hate him, the King was a legend, infusing the blues with rockabilly and country and bringing it to Americans with a hipness and sexuality never seen before. On the day Elvis turned thirty-one, a boy named Andrew was born to David and Marin Wood in Columbus, Mississippi, a scant sixty-two miles south of Presley's birthplace in Tupelo. Eleven years later, Presley passed away at his home in Memphis at forty-two. Autopsies revealed that he had no fewer than ten different narcotics in his system at the time of his death. Though his popularity was waning, he was still the top concert draw of 1977, an amazing feat considering he died that year and only toured for five months.

Andrew Wood, however, never got the chance to see his popularity wane, as he died of a heroin overdose in 1990 at age twenty-four. Wood probably would never have become as popular as Elvis, nor would his band Mother Love Bone. For posterity, all we have is one album, mountains of stories, and lots of promises and speculation. In life, Wood wanted to start a revolution that harkened back to the sixties; in death, he kick-started a phenomenon that defined the closing years of the millennium. Clearly, no matter what was going to happen to Andrew Wood, he was going to make an impact and leave a lasting impression.

When he was just eighteen years old, Wood formed Malfunkshun with his brother Kevin and drummer Regan Hagar. Often considered one of grunge's forefathers (they were included on the *Deep Six* compilation–the Holy Grail of Seattle grunge), Malfunkshun immediately became a massive local hit. They were the sort of band that other bands came out to see, which is why they became close with so many of the other musicians in town and often collaborated with them.

Malfunkshun remains one of grunge's dirty little secrets. For an entire genre built around not only avoiding the bloated theatricality of rock stardom but also regularly expressing hatred for those who trafficked in that sort of pomp, Malfunkshun seemed like the epitome of everything grunge rockers later grew to hate (at least publicly). Their songs certainly fell into the correct idiom, as they were chock-full of hard-driving riffs, but the twist was in the presentation. For one thing, each band member took on an alter ego. Kevin Wood became known as Kevinstein, and Regan Hagar was called Thundarr. Though they took the characters seriously, dressing appropriately for concerts and acting generally like larger versions of themselves, they could not hold a candle to the level of commitment Andrew Wood had to his character, L'Andrew the Love Child. Often clad in over-the-top outfits, complete with feather boas, L'Andrew was a glossy, glammy rock god who resembled Skid Row front man Sebastian Bach but most clearly channeled Freddie Mercury.

Wood's bombast highlighted one of the heaviest influences of grunge that is rarely mentioned in conversation. While most people point to the punk influences or the metal influences, seventies stadium rock had as much to do with the grunge sound as anything, and Andrew Wood's embracing of Steven Tyler's rock-and-roll persona is the prime example of that. Many bands' embracing of seventies riffs, hooks, and solos (most notably Pearl Jam's and Soundgarden's) was typically wrapped in other influences, but Wood brought the theatricality of those bands to the forefront.

Malfunkshun shows were as much about Wood's appearance and stage banter as they were about music. This was convenient, because Malfunkshun was not a very good band. Wood was by far the most compelling force in the mix, and the songs are neither catchy for their hooks nor memorable for their bombast. In fact, Malfunkshun's contributions are the weakest of all the *Deep Six* bands, but even on those recordings, you can tell Wood was an entirely different animal than anyone else involved.

His stage persona was sabotaged by his actual personality, however; in real life, Wood was terribly shy, and relied heavily on drugs to get over that. He did a stint in rehab as early as 1985, but by the time Malfunkshun broke up in 1988, his drug problems were escalating. Still, he managed to continue making music and formed what was one of the most short-lived but also most important bands of the grunge era.

Mother Love Bone was birthed in late 1988 by Wood, guitarist Stone Gossard, and bassist Jeff Ament. The latter two had come from Green River and would eventually form Pearl Jam, and they brought in second guitarist Bruce Fairweather (also formerly of Green River, later of Love Battery) and drummer Greg Gilmore (a cohort of superproducer Jack Endino) to round out the quintet. Though their time was short, the band managed to make quite an impression, as well as providing Ament and Gossard with an incubator that allowed their Pearl Jam concepts to gestate.

When people try to put the sound of grunge into words, they often try to think of a combination of Nirvana and Pearl Jam, but the band they end up describing sounds a lot like Mother Love Bone. The punk influence was present, as the band's simple structures and sped-up rhythms illustrated. The metal influence was also there, though not nearly as pronounced as Soundgarden's metal leanings. But mostly they manage to take the sound of Zeppelin- and Aerosmith-esque arena rock and mutate it into something that doesn't sound like anything else. It was certainly not mainstream, but it could sound at home on the radio. Mother Love Bone hit on a delicate musical chemistry that was damn near perfect.

The only music Mother Love Bone left behind was the proper album *Apple* (released after Wood's death) and a self-titled compilation (sometimes referred to as *Stardog Champion*) that combines tracks from *Apple* with a handful of takes from their EP, *Shine*. Though Mother Love Bone was only a band for two years, their sound was tremendously evolved, as though they had been a functioning unit for much longer.

In all of Mother Love Bone's music, you can hear Pearl Jam starting to develop. "This Is Shangrila" has the same kind of jangly, cascading guitar riff that made up the cornerstones of songs such as "State of Love and Trust," while the epic ballad "Chloe Dancer/Crown of Thorns" not only is a nod to the theatricality of Meat Loaf–esque ballads of yesteryear but also hints at high-drama Pearl Jam tunes such as "Release" and "Yellow Leadbetter."

Mother Love Bone was by far the biggest band in Seattle during their tenure, as they had a built-in following from both Green River and Malfunkshun fans. Their live shows are the stuff of legend, because they were showcases not only for the band's excellent songs but also for Wood's loose-cannon attitude and performance style. So great was the buzz that they were able to sign a major-label deal based on those shows and their self-released EP, *Shine*. The band was never able to enjoy the spoils of their success, however, as Wood died on March 19, 1990, (just a few weeks shy of the album's release date) of a cereberal hemorrhage brought on by an overdose of heroin. As with many fallen rock idols before him, drugs contributed a great deal to who he was both personally and professionally and ultimately led to his undoing. He was only twenty-four years old but still managed to leave quite an impression on the rock community and inspired the best supergroup of the grunge era: Temple of the Dog.

Mother Love Bone broke ground in the Seattle scene, both sonically and philosophically, setting up a number of precedents that other bands followed closely once the scene exploded. Of course, Wood's was the biggest death in the close-knit Seattle rock community until the one-two punch of Kurt Cobain's and Hole's Kristen Pfaff's deaths in 1994. Considering that Wood died in 1990 and Cobain in '94, their deaths essentially bookend the peak of the grunge era. When the scene is bookended by death, then death will no doubt color the music created within it. There's a reason that so many of those grunge songs sound so depressing.

But while many of the musicians involved in the grunge scene felt that specter of death in real time, the fact that Pearl Jam was formed after an overdose and the scene began to implode because of a suicide will forever give people the *perception* that Seattle was ensconced in a culture of death. After Kurt's suicide, a lot of his lyrics suddenly had new meanings. Kurt did not write: "And I swear that I don't have a gun" (from "Come as You Are") knowing that it would be ironic later, but fans and writers did become fixated on the fact that Cobain had made so many references to firearms in his lyrics and nobody had really noticed it before. Lyrically speaking, that irony is what Kurt is more known for now than any of his other imagery.

Courtney Love ran into a similar problem when her band Hole released *Live Through This.* Because that album came out only a week after her husband's death, it was immediately processed and interpreted as an album directed at Cobain's suicide, even though those songs were written and recorded well before Kurt died. The frustrating thing is that some of those songs do actually sound like they could have been written as a reaction to the suicide. Love's line "They get what they want, and they never want it again" (from "Violet") could *easily* function as a reaction to her husband's untimely passing. Of course that makes no logical sense, but time lines tend to fall by the wayside when people are trying to put social histories together. Consequently, Love's album will always bear the burden of Kurt's death.

BESIDES CONTRIBUTING to the culture of death (or at least the *perceived* culture of death—and remember that historically speaking, perception is everything), Mother Love Bone also stood out from the pack because they were careerist. While Mark Arm formed Mudhoney as an all-encompassing expression of his musical vision, Stone Gossard and Jeff Ament wanted to be rock stars, and Mother Love Bone was designed to take them there. They didn't record an EP just to get it into indie record stores; they did it so they could court the attention of major labels. Despite the fact that grunge rockers, fans, and writers sought to maintain as much indie credibility and integrity as possible, nobody turned their noses up at Mother Love Bone. Indeed, whenever any of those bands broke out, they were never considered sellouts. Of course, the people from the scene knew the trials and tribulations of the band members, and since they had been playing music in Seattle for nearly a decade, the yearning for a little success was justified. But people on the outside were less aware of the background stories, so they were unfairly judging bands for which they had no context. Pearl Jam was often accused of being careerist, but rarely by people inside of Seattle. Unfortunately, Kurt Cobain was one of the people who lobbed that accusation at Vedder and company, so they will always be a considered a little ethically loose because Kurt declared them so (even though he recanted his anti–Pearl Jam statements later).

Ironically, Pearl Jam *was* careerist, as was Mother Love Bone. But both those bands earned their careerism, and therein lay the disconnect. Bands were not shunned for wanting to be famous, but *new* bands were. That's why the bands that formed to jump on the bandwagon were so viciously attacked by the core community. But since they were attacking those bands when the rest of the world was paying attention, the perception was that grunge fans were fickle and expected their bands to play down their rock-star tendencies and remain small. Interestingly, Pearl Jam *did* actively get smaller after the release of *Vs.* when they decided to shun videos and public exposure, but even that seemed to some like a too-calculated beg for relevance through martyrdom. Eddie Vedder could never buy a break, and it would have been interesting to see whether or not Andrew Wood would have received the same amount of ire for his rock-star ambitions.

ANDREW WOOD'S death wasn't just about the end of a band or the mourning of a city or the coming together of a new project. Rather, it was the final gasp for a dying breed. Wood lived a hard-rock lifestyle, and when he died he did it as a cautionary tale. He gave an outlet to a lot of musicians and inspired even more, but he also unknowingly started grunge down the path to destruction. Suddenly everything was more serious. In Seattle, it wasn't just about music or business anymore—it was about life and death. The serious era was about to begin, and it was time to do something meaningful or disappear forever. The battle lines were clearly drawn, and a kid from suburban Washington took aim.

Happiness Is a Warm Gun

NIRVANA. THE VERY MENTION OF THE BAND'S NAME CONJURES UP a mother lode of associations, recollections, images, and emotions. Unless you lived on Mars during the early 1990s, you knew exactly who Kurt Cobain was and why his band was loud, awesome, and important. Artistically and aesthetically, their work is still being evaluated, but love them or hate them, Nirvana *meant* something, and not just to their fans—Kurt Cobain, Krist Novoselic, and Dave Grohl transcended being simply a band and wandered into "phenomenon" status, an area of the rock-and-roll pantheon reserved for very few groups. Elvis is there. So are the Beatles. Dylan keeps a residence. Bruce Springsteen knows the grounds. Led Zeppelin wanders in and out. Nirvana broke in during their brief tenure in the spotlight, and no band has joined them among the immortals since then.

Everybody agrees that Nirvana was *Great*, with a capital *G*. But was Nirvana really any *good*?

It's a reasonable thing to get caught up in, but over a decade after Nirvana's demise the band is spoken about in such hallowed tones that many people often forget that Nirvana even released records. Normally, this isn't all that problematic. When you've gone beyond simply being a band to being a full-fledged cultural landmark, nobody ever debates your merit anymore. Sure, there are people who prefer *Sgt. Pepper's* to *Abbey Road*, but there are no really great debates about which Beatles album is the best—it's universally agreed that it's *all* excellent. The Beatles represented so much more than simply four guys playing music that those rock songs (or at least the quality of them) stopped mattering. The music remained excellent, but the Beatles' success (and, more important, their historical significance) ceased to hinge on the quality of their music. In the end, their shoes and haircuts became *way* more essential than "Penny Lane."

As time goes by, Nirvana has built up a similar mystique. While their scope was nowhere near that of the Beatles (they simply weren't around long enough), Nirvana (and Kurt in particular) represented something that was much larger than their music, videos, or concerts. Whenever anybody mentions the words "grunge" or "alternative," Nirvana is the touchstone band from which all other images and sounds are derived. People's grandmothers knew who Kurt Cobain was, and those same grandmothers recognized that he was more than just a musician. He was an icon. He was a legend. He was a living deity.

Ironically, Nirvana had almost nothing to do with the other bands they are commonly associated with whenever people talk about the grunge era. Sonically, they were the only band involved in the scene that *sounded* like they had punk influences. There was no complicated riffing or bulldozing structures like on the records cut by Soundgarden and Pearl Jam. Nirvana's songs were tight, compact, noisy, and to the point, especially on *Nevermind* (despite Kurt's repeated dismissal of that album as being "too slick"). In fact, Nirvana had almost an independent set of influences entirely—Cobain was known to have worshiped at the altar of the

Pixies, Scratch Acid, Flipper, Daniel Johnston, and other acts not typically associated with the grunge sound.

Unlike most of the other bands from the grunge scene, there is no point in debating the importance of Nirvana. They are important. No rational argument can be made that states that Kurt Cobain's band was irrelevant in any way, shape, or form. They will always be remembered, so the real issue becomes specifically *how* they will be remembered. Will they be remembered as a band that was complicated and full of contradictions and simultaneously difficult to love and easy to adore? Or will they simply be remembered as the guys who sang "Smells Like Teen Spirit"?

Amazingly, both of those adjudications might be correct.

GOING OVER the biography of Nirvana serves entirely no purpose for two reasons. First, their story has been told both repeatedly and better in a number of other places (most notably in Michael Azerrad's biography *Come as You Are* and the Cobain-focused tome *Heavier than Heaven* by Charles R. Cross). Their story is so straightforward that it's almost apocryphal and falls into so many rock-and-roll clichés that it's almost become a piece of mythology. Even if you don't know the story of Nirvana, you sort of already do.

The other reason that there is no point setting up Nirvana's backstory is that it doesn't do anybody any good. Since they have graduated to the particular level of historical import that befits so few bands, their early years no longer serve them (or anybody else) in any meaningful way, especially considering the band has been defunct for so long. A lot of people go on and on about the early Beatles shows at German clubs and about Pete Best, but those stories do not affect who the Beatles are now in any way. Historical details don't matter to legends—when you are immortal, the past becomes wholly irrelevant. There is only the present and the future. Nirvana only exists as an undying series of sounds and images, and stories about growing up in suburban Washington and sleeping on floors and touring with Tad and firing drummers don't affect those images or sounds at all, so they are irrelevant to the discussion of the band's historical significance.

What is relevant, however, is in what manner they will be remembered. Since their demise (and specifically because of the manner in which that demise occurred), a lot of presumptions have been made about Nirvana's legacy and their place in history. But when future civilizations comb through the wreckage of our world, they will only be able to judge what Nirvana has left behind.

So what did Nirvana leave behind?

Ask anybody what the most essential Nirvana album is, and most will say it is *Nevermind.* The cultural significance of *Nevermind* cannot be understated; in fact, despite the years of acclaim, it still may not receive the respect it deserves. As a piece of music, it's probably a little overrated, as while some of the songs are legendary and deservedly so ("Smells Like Teen Spirit" and "Come as You Are" among them), the bulk of the album sometimes seems suspiciously like filler. An album can absolutely be declared great even with a couple of dud songs on it, but the problem is that the songs on *Nevermind* that aren't legendary look even more minor when put side by side with the ones that are. Love it or hate it, "Territorial Pissings" will always seem like a throwaway tune when put next to "In Bloom."

So *Nevermind* is slightly overrated musically, but since Nirvana is legendary, then the content of the album has little to do with its legacy. With that in mind, what else makes *Nevermind* so important?

Obviously, Nirvana was not the first "alternative" band and *Nevermind* wasn't the first alternative album, but Nirvana was the first alternative band to release an album that mattered. Certainly

R.E.M. had been putting out quality albums that were slowly building momentum, but *Nevermind* beat their big breakout success, *Out of Time*, to store shelves by a month. Of course, Pearl Jam's *Ten* was released before *Nevermind*, but that album didn't start to matter until "Jeremy" took off (see chapter 5).

Being first doesn't necessarily make you more important—just ask Leif Eriksson. Nirvana had a lot more going for it than timing, and it had everything to do with their front man. Kurt Cobain was a strange, loud, angry, sensitive, misunderstood guy, and he also had an undefinable sexiness that said as much about his antifame aesthetic as it did about his bone structure. It wasn't just that "Smells Like Teen Spirit" was an incredible song that had a killer hook and mysterious lyrics and exploited the soft verse/loud chorus dynamic better than any other song in history. Having a song on the radio is never enough—the audience needs to experience the artist presented before them. Rock fans needed to see Cobain and watch him do what he does. They needed a venue. They needed a video.

It is for this reason that the premiere of the clip for "Smells Like Teen Spirit" is one of the most important events in rock history. Grunge existed prior to the Samuel Bayer–directed short, but until it was unveiled, grunge was simply a bunch of guys who dressed warm, took drugs together, and made dissonant music. "Smells Like Teen Spirit"—and, more specifically, that legendary video—made grunge into a phenomenon, for better or for worse.

The "Smells Like Teen Spirit" clip is fairly uncomplicated. Inspired by a 1979 film about teenage rebellion called *Over the Edge* that Cobain was fond of—and which also supposedly inspired the video for Smashing Pumpkins' "1979"—it takes place inside a heavily art-directed high school gymnasium. It's the pep rally from hell, and Nirvana is the house band. There is a team of cheerleaders with the anarchy symbol on their chests doing robotic routines, and there's a group of disaffected youths sitting in some bleachers. The video is fairly uneventful—it's basically Nirvana playing the song in a gymnasium while the weird cheerleaders do their thing. But toward the end, the disaffected youths sitting in the bleachers charge onto the floor to slam dance in slow motion and destroy the set. The clip ends with a far-too-close-up shot of Cobain screaming, "A denial," into the camera as the feedback fades around him. For most of the video, the band is shot at a distance and Cobain's hair and the shadows in the gym mask most of the singer's features anyway. Kurt's face isn't revealed until that final shot, and by getting close enough to count his pores Bayer made Kurt into an instant icon. Here was a guy who was emotional and intense but also rugged and attractive. It was an incredible combination, and by looking into Kurt's eyes as he sang the closing lines of "Smells Like Teen Spirit," prospective Nirvana fans became Kurt acolytes in a matter of seconds.

Of course, there's a great deal of irony there. Kurt Cobain was as antifame as anybody in the grunge scene, and despite the fact that Eddie Vedder has admitted that Mudhoney always acted as the fame cop in Seattle, Kurt was the philosophical judge, jury, and executioner when it came to overexposure. But it's a fairly amazing thing that a guy who desperately wanted to remain anonymous became an instantaneous icon through the medium of music videos. "Smells Like Teen Spirit" was the first of many genius marketing ploys when it came to Nirvana, as it successfully packaged a songwriter and a band who were largely considered to be countercultural as a group of young guys who were meant to be embraced as mainstream rock and rollers (Nirvana would later send up this dichotomy in the very funny video for "In Bloom").

"Smells Like Teen Spirit" is so full of alt-rock video tropes that it seems like a four-minute cliché, but in 1991 they were revolutionary. One of the things that stands out is the fact that Kurt is wearing a flannel shirt. Soon flannel would become a generic identifier for all the kids who were embracing "slacker" culture, but that wasn't true when "Smells Like Teen Spirit" was made. But another memorable set of images from the video is the shots of the disaffected youths sitting in the bleachers. Videos where young people rebel and destroy things were nothing new (just about every Twisted Sister video followed that format), but it's actually more important to notice what the kids *aren't* doing—they aren't giving a damn. They look bored, even as the band rocks out in front of them. It's as though *they* could have written the heavily affected lyric "Here we are now, entertain us" from "Smells Like Teen Spirit." Though they were just extras on a video shoot, that group of kids also defined what it was to be a Nirvana fan. According to "Smells Like Teen Spirit," their fans didn't even care that a giant rock band was playing in front of them. It was an antistar attitude that the band carried, and they passed it on to their (fictional) fans. Later that apathy, which led to a certain sense of egalitarianism, became a cornerstone of the grunge attitude. Grunge didn't care about stardom. It didn't care about being on the cover of magazines. It was one gigantic shrug. It was revolutionary, but it also set everybody up for failure. Revolutions need enthusiasm.

Naturally, part of this problem was inspired by the band itself. Cobain was heavily influenced by punk rock not just sonically but also in attitude, which is 98 percent of punk rock anyway. Though the prevailing opinion among alternative rockers was that they did not have any interest in being famous, Kurt was one of the few who seemed to mean it all the time. He always played ball for the sake of his livelihood and the livelihoods of his band members, but Kurt loathed awards shows and had little tolerance for MTV. Nirvana was constantly on the network, but it was often on Kurt's own terms. When the band was first breaking and before shows like *Alternative Nation* had been established, MTV put Nirvana in the same place they put the rest of their loud rock bands: on the metalhead-centric *Headbanger's Ball*, which was hosted by Riki Rachtman. In one of the most notorious and iconic segments in MTV history, Cobain showed up on the show wearing a dress. "It's *Headbanger's Ball*," he explained on-air. "I thought I'd wear a gown." Here was the most aggro, alpha-male show MTV had to offer, and the guest of the day entirely subverted the concept with skewed sexual politics. It's no mystery that though *Headbanger's Ball* ran until 1994 (and was then revived in 2003), Kurt's "invasion" of the metal world certainly announced that metal was done.

Cobain was a master at scenarios like that. It would be easy to call Kurt a hypocrite because he always talked about how much he loathed fame and the trappings of celebrity culture but always seemed to be on TV or making headlines. Plus, Kurt was always vocal about other bands' embracing of rock stardom. The argument is a fairly easy one to make, as Kurt was not just the leader of a band but also a figurehead who represented a movement, a critical darling, and a wild commercial success. Being on top of the mountain makes it quite easy to say, "We don't care about fame," because Nirvana *had* become the biggest band in the universe. Kurt sometimes came across like a disaffected rich kid in that sense—he was a guy who had everything and condemned most of the spoils showered upon him, but when push came to shove he still allowed it to happen. If Kurt was really serious about shunning fame, why wouldn't he take the Ian MacKaye approach and actively limit the scope and exposure of his band?

But Kurt was honest to a fault and often owned up to the irony of his situation. It doesn't completely absolve him of what could be construed as his hypocrisies, but a little bit of self-awareness often goes an awfully long way. That's what truly made Kurt Cobain special: He was an impressive songwriter, was extremely intelligent, and had an undeniable mysterious sexiness about him, but what set him apart was that he was the first completely self-omniscient rock star. At every moment in his career, Kurt knew *exactly* what everything he said and did would mean to *everybody*, especially after he made the crossover to being a pop star. Part of it was knowing his audience and part of it was knowing how to manipulate the press, but Kurt went on a remarkable run of being completely in control of his own destiny and how he was perceived by the world at large.

For example, Kurt butted heads with MTV at the 1992 Video Music Awards. Nirvana was booked to play the show, and Kurt wanted to play a new tune called "Rape Me," which would later appear on *In Utero* and become one of the most famous and beloved songs in the entire Nirvana catalog. MTV hesitated, partially because they wanted the band to play their massive hit "Smells Like Teen Spirit" and partially because they naturally were nervous about airing a song called "Rape Me." Eventually, Kurt and MTV came to a compromise and decided to play "Lithium." However, when the band began to play the live telecast, Kurt played the opening riff of "Rape Me," much to the horror of the MTV crew running the show (interestingly enough, Kurt's "Rape Me" intro was initially misconstrued as a tease of "Smells Like Teen Spirit," as the former's riff is a simple inversion of the latter's). It only lasted a few seconds, though, as Kurt then led the band through a surging version of "Lithium," whose conclusion saw Kurt destroy the band's equipment and Krist Noveselic toss his bass up in the air only to have it hit him on the head when it came back down. Not surprisingly, it's one of the most incredible performances by a band in the history of the VMAs.

But here's the rub: When people talk about the 1992 show now, the only thing ever mentioned is the fight between Kurt and MTV and Kurt's "Rape Me" rope-a-dope. Whether it was conscious or not (and it seems like it would have to be), Kurt knew exactly how his actions would be perceived, and though he ultimately didn't get to play the song he wanted to play, he still came out looking like a hero, and MTV, though in the end they got their way, looked absolutely impotent against a shaggy guy from the Pacific Northwest. Kurt ultimately kowtowed, and yet he still looks like a punk-rock hero damning the man at every turn. It's one of the cornerstone stories in the Nirvana mythology, and Kurt made it so.

Just as Johnny Rotten inspired fans to throw things at authority, Ozzy Osbourne inspired fans to embrace Satan, and Vince Neil inspired fans to drink and fuck, Kurt's effect on his followers was profound, but in a very atypical way. Nirvana inspired the same sort of antiauthoritarian philosophy as the punk rockers did, but it was absolutely a more intellectual sort of damn-the-man stance. Kurt was opinionated and self-aware and spoke about things like domestic violence (it's no surprise that both of his bandmates, especially Noveselic, later became involved in various politcal venues). To Kurt's hardcore fans, he made it seem downright awesome to be smart and self-aware. People responded to this in droves, and it was an important part of why Nirvana became huge: Finally, loud music wasn't just for mooks anymore. Kids who were disaffected, smart, and emotional finally had big rock music to call their own, and it was *popular*. Suddenly they hadn't just infiltrated the in crowd—they *were* the in crowd.

This was a liberating thing for a lot of music fans, but ultimately it also might have been the entire movement's undoing. Cobain's heavy use of irony and his generally apathetic demeanor were often misconstrued as cynicism, though philosophically Cobain was more of a skeptic than a cynic. The larger an audience a message reaches, the more confused it can become, and this was no exception. Legions of rock fans saw Cobain and wanted to be like him, so they thought that the best way to become incredibly awesome was to act jaded.

There's nothing inherently wrong with being jaded, as it makes people harder to fool and perhaps makes people analyze ideas more thoroughly. However, it rarely leads to productivity and eventually leads to the dismissal of just about everything. This is a problematic philosophy for a scene, as eventually even the bands that established said scene are ultimately dismissed. It's one of the many reasons bands had a hard time following up their debut singles or albums—by the time they got around to making more music, the coolest thing to do was to hate what you actually loved. Of course, it's true that many of the follow-ups from the era, many of which are discussed elsewhere in this book, also had the unfortunate qualification of being not very good. But the attitude toward bands (and culture at large) certainly didn't help.

Taken in this context, the "Smells Like Teen Spirit" video ended up predicting the entire evolution of the grunge era. The video begins with a loud band playing to disaffected youths, and that crowd becomes inspired by said loud band to rise up and be heard. Ultimately, the disaffected youths turn on the very band that empowered them, destroying it (or at least what it represented) completely. In this sense, Kurt Cobain was an alt-rock Nostradamus who foresaw grunge's end before it really ever got started. Killing your idols can be a great thing, but you always have to be aware of who might be replacing them.

HISTORY HAS been fair to the other members of Nirvana, as it seems like they will be judged based on their own merit and not necessarily on their accomplishments in the band. This seems especially true of drummer Dave Grohl, who to an entire generation of rock fans is the guy who fronts Foo Fighters and who used to be in Nirvana, rather than the other way around. Grohl's group has already had a longer career than Nirvana did, and Foo Fighters has become a radio staple, churning out huge crossover hits such as "Big Me," "Everlong," and "Learn to Fly." He has also become a bit of a rock-and-roll all-star, playing drums on Queens of the Stone Age's breakout hit record, *Songs for the Deaf,* and putting together a metal supergroup called Probot. Grohl has never really been averse to discussing Nirvana, but it seems as though people bring it up less and less as the years go on.

Nirvana bassist Krist Novoselic, who was closer to Cobain than anybody not named Courtney Love, has not quite received the same sort of treatment, especially musically—his post-Nirvana groups Sweet 75 and Eyes Adrift were both forgettable and short-lived. But Krist has made himself into something of a political action figure for aging alt-rockers, even going as far as releasing a book called *Of Grunge and Government: Let's Fix This Broken Democracy!* He even briefly considered a run at being the lieutenant governor of Washington in 2004 but ultimately decided against it. Still, he remains a very visible icon in the Washington State political arena, and though he's still typically identified as "former Nirvana bassist Krist Novoselic," it's a title he embraces and he is aware his rub from Nirvana has helped gain attention for his political causes.

The point is that no matter how much lip service Kurt gave to the sense of camaraderie and collaboration among the three men, Nirvana was Kurt's band, and as the other band members carve out their own niches elsewhere, Nirvana becomes more and more about Kurt and his individual legacy. The legacy of Nirvana is that of Kurt Cobain.

So what is that legacy? More specifically, when Kurt shuffled off this mortal coil, how did he leave the music world that he no doubt changed forever?

One of the most important things to remember is that Kurt Cobain is probably the most famous and influential punk of all time. His band didn't always play music that sounded like the traditional accepted version of punk (like the Clash, Sex Pistols, or Ramones), but even when rolling in limousines or selling out stadiums in Europe, Kurt Cobain embodied the punk ethos by acting like he was no better than a common rock-and-roll street urchin.

Of course, Kurt *was* better than the average bear, not just as a songwriter and a performer but also as a thinker. One of Cobain's greatest gifts to the universe of rock was that he was smarter than just about everybody, or at least wanted everybody to *believe* he was smarter. Cobain wasn't overeducated—he didn't spend time at Harvard for fun like Weezer front man Rivers Cuomo, nor did he have a Ph.D. like Offspring singer Dexter Holland—but did make it seem supercool to act brainy. Since Kurt represented outcasts, the smart kids embraced him as a representative. For a time, he was the biggest rock star in the world, and he passively defended the honor of physics club members everywhere.

One of grunge's main sources of popularity was the sense that it was loud music for smart people. Everybody wants to rock, but not everybody wants to have to do it as insipidly as eighties metal gods did. That's not to say that Nirvana albums were any smarter than *Dr. Feelgood*, but *In Utero* certainly projected an air of sophistication, as though you had to be a little smarter (or at least aspire to be a little smarter) in order to like it. That's not to say that everybody picking up a Nirvana record was a brain surgeon, but even the mooks could *feel* smarter by listening to Kurt, because that was the tone he projected.

Rock critics loved this—many of the greats still speak wistfully of the grunge era, not only because they are attached to an extremely anticommercial music that suddenly became commercial but also because it allowed them to really delve into the science of criticism.

Since guys such as Kurt Cobain and Eddie Vedder (and even Gavin Rossdale) presented themselves and their bands with a certain amount of intellectual sophistication, there was an implicit invitation to really break their records down. Overanalysis ran rampant throughout the early nineties. Critics and fans picked away at every note and lyric in order to find the deep hidden meanings in the music. People made all sorts of assumptions about Pearl Jam's "mamasan" tracks, while conspiracy theorists filled up Internet message boards with Cobain lyrics after his suicide, claiming he had been leaving messages all along. A song like Alice in Chains' "Rooster" seemed pretty straightforward, but it was pored over as though it were Elizabethan poetry. That didn't happen with Poison albums, and it happened much less when bands like Papa Roach came to town later.

There are two possible stances to take on this particular issue. The first (and less cynical) is that these guys actually were smarter and deeper and more articulate and their music was intellectually stimulating in ways that attracted a more attuned listener. The second stance is that it's possible that those same fans were simply grafting the collegiate intellectual discourse they had become familiar with onto something that seemed like it merited analysis. After all, the guys in Pearl Jam and Alice in Chains had no problems with divulging the actual meanings of their songs, and there was a secret fear among fans that Kurt Cobain's oft-analyzed lyrics were actually meaningless (people often forget that the chorus to one of Cobain's greatest songs is the word "yeah" repeated fourteen times).

Perhaps Kurt simply had such a profound level of self-awareness that it always seemed like he was terribly perceptive and insightful when in reality he only knew a whole lot about himself. But even if that was true, it would still have been a major coup for the state of pop music, as rock fans never had a brainier figurehead, or at least a guy who seemed really smart. The only other front man who appears to have mastered this is Bono, who seems superintelligent but might very well be a complete idiot. However, his actual intellectual acumen is almost irrelevent, because he is *perceived* as a brilliant mind. Rock fans react to perception—in fact, sometimes that's all rock and roll is. Ozzy Osbourne had an incredibly long and successful career because people thought he was the world's foremost worshiper of Satan. Ozzy never really prayed to the devil (at least not on purpose), but the very suggestion of it made it so. The same principle applies to Kurt Cobain: He never proved himself to be a brilliant guy, but his image was such that he will be remembered as an intelligent dude.

Rock fans in the early nineties went right along with it, engaging Kurt and the rest of the grunge rockers in a sort of intellectual discourse over music and the various issues that the bands stood for. Like Christian rock bands, whose fans just really want to pray after the show, grunge rockers invited a whole different level of fan interaction. A keen sense of perception was king, which is why every serious rock fan went around talking like a music critic for three-quarters of a decade. The idea that you could see into the music and make observations suddenly became an important part of being a fan, and Kurt Cobain's band was the most analyzed of these supposedly "smart" rock bands.

This sense of overanalysis changed the way pop music was consumed forever. In today's landscape, every band, performer, and song is picked apart and scrutinized over in great detail, often before the album officially comes out. The Internet has been a great catalyst for this, as all sorts of people have been able to build communities around discussing obscure Smiths singles and the machinations of Beyoncé's songwriting process. All of this, of course, is counterintuitive to the whole concept of pop music, which is supposed to be a visceral experience and not necessarily an intellectual exercise. There is such thing as taking this stuff too far—while there are ideas and concepts to be analyzed in hip-hop, trying to draw hidden meaning from Dipset songs just seems like a massive waste of time. But the Internet didn't create this generation of pseudoprofound pop critics. It is just a medium through which those ideas can be focused and those thinkers can communicate. It's merely a piece of technology that brought people together who were already thinking the same thing but didn't know it. They learned that people everywhere were taking rock songs way too seriously— a trick they learned from growing up with *Nevermind* and the rest of the brainy noisemakers of the early nineties. Heady exploration can be a good thing, even an excellent thing, but because grunge songs were so loud and often so radio-friendly, it was assumed that *anything* could be given philosophical weight if considered enough. But there's a fine line between "Lithium" and, say, Busta Rhymes' "Cocaina," and it's mostly Kurt's fault that the line faded away a long time ago.

KURT COBAIN took his own life on or around April 5, 1994. Though there are several parties who believe that he was murdered, no substantial evidence of this has ever been brought forward, and the discrepancies in the reports filed by the Seattle Police Department are likely the result of shoddy cop work and little else. In fact, the film that sought to present a conclusive conspiracy theory about Kurt's supposed "murder," *Kurt & Courtney*, is so loose that it ends up passively making a case *against* the conspiracy.

Though Cobain's death has certainly been romanticized, suicide is actually one of the least romantic of all deaths, especially of rock-and-roll deaths. Had Cobain overdosed on heroin or crashed a car or drunk himself to death, it would be considered far more romantic in the rock-and-roll sense. After all, those are the types of ends that claimed rock legends Jim Morrison, Janis Joplin, and fellow Seattleite Jimi Hendrix (though it's probably no coincidence that like the latter two, Cobain also died a "mysterious" death). Somehow, the rock community is able to accept deaths via overdose or neglect as though they are simply written off as the acceptable fallout of the rock-and-roll lifestyle. Rock stars (especially those who play big-time arena rock) are almost *expected* to OD, which is partially why people are still obsessed with Ozzy Osbourne even though he hasn't released a decent piece of music in two decades: Nobody can believe that dude is still upright.

But suicide is a totally different situation. It's an active choice. It's a specific decision. Even if that choice is made under the influence of chemicals in the body, it's still an incredible act of will. And though some people are slow to admit it because it sounds callous, there is a definite level of cowardice in offing yourself. Certainly Cobain had reasons for doing it, but once the initial shock wears off, the question of "why" sets in, and when people ponder that question, they are inherently suggesting that the person in question not only had excellent reasons to live but also had terrible reasons to die. Cobain left behind a wife and a young child. Even considering the amount of physical and psychological pain he was in, there's no doubt that he was weak.

Of course, people don't want to believe their heroes are pansies, or if they go down, fans want to know they went down swinging. Though Cobain killed himself in a dramatic fashion that shocked the world, it was more of a whimper of an end than a bang.

It wasn't anywhere near the shift in tone that occurred in this country after John F. Kennedy was shot, but it's a similar ballpark, as Cobain's death contributed to a dramatic attitude adjustment not just in rock music but all over pop culture. Cobain's success (along with that of the rest of the Seattle grunge rockers) proved that even sloppy slackers could make it big if they believed enough in their art, but the suicide was a sour end to that dream. Somewhere somebody was saying, "I told you so." The grunge years always seemed too good to be true, and as it turned out, that was pretty much the case.

Looking forward from 1994, the next dominant genre of mainstream rock became rap-metal (which later evolved into the broader but no less aggro "nü metal"). Nü metal was pure aggression— bands like Korn and Staind sang mostly about their unbridled rage at their parents, their teachers, their ex-girlfriends, and whoever else happened to be around. There was almost no introspection anywhere, and the uncomfortable misogyny that seemed to be played for over-the-top goofiness so often in the eighties now felt uncomfortably real. Kids who had come of age with Nirvana tuned in to MTV one day and saw their hero had taken his own life. Their reaction? Raw, unadulterated anger. And who could blame them? According to Cobain's actions, the reward for believing in yourself and staying true to who you were was a lifetime of mental and physical anguish, escapable only through self-sacrifice. Bands such as Limp Bizkit were raging against that machine, promoting a lifestyle that would never end in tragedy like Cobain's. That's not to suggest that those bands were *only* rioting because of Cobain's suicide, but it had to have been a factor in their approach to rock music.

But it didn't just extend to the bands. In order for it to have become a phenomenon, the fans had to have been onboard as well, and they certainly had their brains scrambled by the news of Cobain's death. There has always been a lot of talk about how no other star or band "stepped up" to fill the void left by Cobain, but the listeners were just as guilty. They didn't want to side with somebody new because their other spokesman had turned out to be a dud. He certainly did the job while he was alive, but his legacy would always be tainted by the nature of his death. Rock fans (and especially *young* rock fans) initially felt the sadness and shock that come with a death such as Kurt's, but the mourners eventually became jaded. It's hard to really pinpoint it, but there was a latent sense of cynicism that bubbled under the surface in the late nineties but erupted around the turn of the millennium. If you were a fourteen-year-old Nirvana fan in '94, that means by 2000 you were a twenty-year-old who felt a lot of millennial tension, watched the dot-com bubble burst, and didn't trust the government. It's an entire generation of kids who took the reactionary lyrics to "Serve the Servants" take on teenage angst to heart: "Now I'm bored and old." That twenty-first-century malaise that all the newscasters talked about after September 11 snapped everyone out of it was no accident. Again, Cobain's death didn't send all of America's youth on a downward spiral, but it certainly contributed to a culture focused on failed heroes. Naturally, Cobain never intended any of this, but the fact remains: Kurt had a lot of people to answer to, whether he liked it or not. By committing suicide, he may have solidified his place in the all-time rock pantheon and elevated Nirvana's status from a groundbreaking band to a legendary band, but he made rock culture a whole lot more problematic in the process. Had he lived, everyone would have had to deal with the aging Cobain, likely putting out esoteric folk albums or trying his hand at psych-rock or prog. But that's the sort of fall fans can handle—they're conditioned for it, considering how often it happens. Suicide is a whole different story. Whether or not Kurt knew it (and it's possible that he could have, considering his gift for insight), his suicide would be the second most defining aspect of his life. "Smells Like Teen Spirit" was so large that nothing will ever overtake it, but the dark reality of his end is always waiting in the wings to eclipse that song on the historical importance scale. As we go forward, it will be interesting to note whether or not "Teen Spirit" can even outlive death.

NIRVANA'S SAVING grace will likely forever be "Smells Like Teen Spirit." It was a hugely popular song that also acted as the introduction to a revolution and a sound track to the thoughts, wishes, and fears of a generation. There's no question that they were a problematic band and that Cobain was a conflicted and difficult rock star. There's no question that their legacy will likely always be just slightly overblown. There's no question that *Nevermind* will always be overrated and that *In Utero* will remain slightly underrated and most of their other work will be fetishized beyond all logic—witness the 2004 box set *With the Lights Out*, a collection of outtakes and b-sides that culls together songs that are mostly terrible. But they had Kurt Cobain's voice on them, and that will make them indispensable.

But none of that matters. *That's* how big a band Nirvana was. Not just in sales but also in influence and importance. "Smells Like Teen Spirit" didn't just sell a lot of albums. Rather, it convinced people to buy into a lifestyle. Musically, Nirvana was probably the least interesting (or the least complex) of the "Big Four," but nobody burned themselves in the memories of the collective conscious quite like Kurt Cobain.

When those kids rioted in the "Teen Spirit" video, they weren't just slam dancing—they were stomping all over several decades of rock history and blowing the doors open for the guys on the fringe to steal the spotlight and call the shots for a while. Cobain's culture of uncool cool is indestructible and will remain so until the end of time.

CHAPTER 5

—

PEARL JAM

Earnest Goes to Number One

IN THE AFTERMATH OF ANDREW WOOD'S TRAGIC DEATH, STONE Gossard and Jeff Ament became deeply ensconced in Temple of the Dog. But that was simply meant to be a tribute and nothing more. The band would not tour and initially didn't even have a distributor for the album. This was totally logical at the time. Even though the band would be considered a supergroup only a year later, few people had heard of Soundgarden in 1990 and fewer still were familiar with Mother Love Bone. Chris Cornell, Matt Cameron, and Kim Thayil returned to the confines of Soundgarden, leaving Jeff Ament, Stone Gossard, and Eddie Vedder together in what would become the second most important band of the grunge era and undoubtedly the one with the longest legacy.

Pearl Jam began life shortly after Mother Love Bone called it quits. It seemed obvious that Stone Gossard and Jeff Ament would continue to make music together, as they had been collaborators since the Green River days. Andrew Wood's death did not hinder their creative forces, and if anything the sense of mortality made their drive even greater. In the spring of 1990, they recorded a handful of demos, many of which became songs on their debut, *Ten*. Their friend Matt Cameron (who would join Pearl Jam permanently a decade later) played drums on those original tracks. They were rough, but they were a logical extension of the songs Gossard and Ament had been playing in Mother Love Bone— arena-ready riffs delivered with punk-rock enthusiasm and professional panache.

Also included in the sessions for those demos was second guitarist Mike McCready. Though he was an old high school friend of Gossard's and they both played guitar, the demo tape was their first collaboration. McCready had already attempted a bid at rock stardom, most notably as a guitarist in a metal band called Shadow, which formed when he was still in high school. After a thirteen-month stay in Los Angeles trying to break in, Shadow returned to Seattle and broke up shortly thereafter, leaving McCready without a band. For a short time, he hung up his guitar. He went back to school briefly but soon became obsessed with Stevie Ray Vaughan, and McCready quickly was back on the ax.

Inspired by the stylings of Vaughan, McCready formed a psychedelic blues band called Love Chile. Though they broke up within a couple of months, they stayed together long enough to play for an audience that included Gossard, who was impressed by McCready's guitar work and invited him to jam and eventually join up with him and Ament. McCready came armed—one of the first things he showed Gossard was a riff he had been working on that would be the basis for "Alive." He also had the beginnings of the song that would later become *Ten*'s cornerstone ballad, "Black."

With competent songwriters, musicians, and a handful of tunes already set to go, all the new band really needed was a front man. Gossard and Ament had been used to the dynamo that was Andrew Wood, and replacing him would be impossible. Still, they knew they needed a guy who would be a showman and who would be able to express himself and own the stage on a level approaching Wood's. Gossard labeled the tapes "GOSSARD DEMOS '91" and circulated them among his friends and connections. In lieu of any sort of packaging, Gossard also sent along basketball cards featuring his favorite player: Mookie Blaylock.

One of those tapes ended up in the hands of Jack Irons, a drummer whom Gossard had known for years. Irons was the original drummer of the Red Hot Chili Peppers before leaving that band in 1988 after the death of original guitarist Hillel Slovak. Irons went on to form Eleven with Alain Johannes, the former front man of a band called What Is This?—which also contained Irons and Slovak. Irons was an L.A. guy who had befriended Gossard and Ament and, since he had already seen success with the Red Hot Chili Peppers, was more familiar with the inner workings of the music business. Plus, Gossard and Ament felt that their songs needed a fresh perspective, one that wasn't already tainted by the building buzz of Seattle.

Irons listened to the songs and handed the tape off to a friend of his, a San Diego surfer and aspiring musician who had befriended Irons over their mutual love of both rock music and nature. Ed Vedder was a gutsy outdoorsman, so much so that his love for forays into the unknown and death-defying leaps (something that would later become a staple of his performance style) earned him the nickname Crazy Eddie.

Vedder immediately fell in love with the three songs on the demo tape and began generating lyrics while surfing. He came up with a high-concept three-part story that could be told over the three tracks on the tape. The first part was about a woman who reveals to her son that the man he has known as his father is not actually his father; his real father is dead, and there is more than a hint of Oedipal undertones between mother and son. The second part told the story of how disturbed the young man had become, leading him to something of a psychotic break. He goes on a killing spree that ends act two. The third and final song, acting as the denouement, is the young man's final thoughts as he is being led to his execution. Those three songs, "Alive," "Once," and "Footsteps," became the cornerstones of Pearl Jam's debut (though "Footsteps" ended up being left off the album and was subsequently used as a b-side to the "Jeremy" single). When Vedder sent the tape back with his lyrics and vocals recorded over Gossard's tracks, he scribbled the word "mamasan" on the tape, which is why these three songs are commonly referred to as the "mamasan trilogy" or the "mamasan tryptic."

When the tape got back to Gossard, he was blown away. He immediately invited Vedder up from San Diego so he could meet him in person and begin to play with him and Ament to see if the chemistry worked. Vedder tried to convince Jack Irons to come with him, as the band was still without a drummer and Irons was a mutual friend to all the band members. Though he would later join the band full-time, Irons did not want to abandon his commitment to Eleven (with whom he would play on three albums) and also did not want to leave his home in Los Angeles, where he had a wife who was expecting their first child.

By the time Eddie got to Seattle, Gossard, Ament, and McCready had already decided to move forward as Mookie Blaylock. The Temple of the Dog sessions were nearly complete, though not so complete that they didn't allow Vedder to record backing vocals for a song called "Hunger Strike." Though the Seattle music community was fairly insular and did not necessarily look kindly on outsiders, Vedder was accepted into the fold almost immediately (mostly because he had Gossard's blessing, which was as good as gold). In fact, it's ironic that Vedder, who now defines Seattle but at the time was an outsider, ended up becoming so emblematic of the city and its music scene. His individual rise was nothing short of meteoric: When Temple of the Dog reconvened almost a year later to shoot the video for "Hunger Strike," Vedder was prominently featured as the band's front man, even though he was little more than a side player during the sessions. Of course, the reason Temple of the Dog got the opportunity to shoot a video in the first place was the success of *Ten*, so it's not surprising that Vedder had suddenly become the center of attention.

Following the completion of the Temple of the Dog album, Mookie Blaylock began working on a new record almost immediately. Many of the songs were already in place—the "mamasan" tracks were ready to go, and McCready and Gossard had developed several other songs since the recording of the first demos. Needing a drummer, they settled on Dave Krusen, a local guy who had a loose, Charlie Watts–inspired sound. Krusen's life in Pearl Jam was short-lived, as he left the band before the release of the first album, citing "family reasons," though he later revealed that a drinking problem also played into his decision. Kreusen found success with Hovercraft (the band fronted by Eddie Vedder's wife, Beth Liebling), grunge bandwagoners Candlebox, and Unified Theory, which contained most of the former members of Blind Melon.

This set up an interesting precedent for Pearl Jam: the revolving door at the drum seat. For one reason or another, the band has gone through four drummers in fifteen years (ironically, they are currently supported on the skins by Matt Cameron, the former Soundgarden drummer who played on the original demos, which technically makes him the original drummer). Usually that level of turnover can drive a wedge between other band members, but the brotherhood of Pearl Jam's four main components is a bond that is seemingly indestructible. In fifteen years, there has been nary a breakup rumor and very few incidents of rock star divaness. If anything, the members of Pearl Jam have underplayed their hand (something that plays into the latter half of their career quite profoundly). It's a situation where the chemistry was absolutely right from the get-go, and it has not been in question since.

MIDWAY THROUGH the sessions for their debut album, Mookie Blaylock decided their name was somewhat ridiculous and opted to change it to the slightly less ridiculous Pearl Jam. The new name was emblematic of Vedder's quick rise to becoming the figurehead of the band, as it was a tribute to his grandmother Pearl and a homemade remedy she used to cook up.

The newly christened band's studio sessions for *Ten* were smooth and efficient, which was no surprise, as the band was made up mostly of professionals who had been in that particular scenario before. That is, except for Vedder. Until that moment, Eddie Vedder had been little more than a poetic surf rat, and now he was the front man of a band, where he would be encouraged—nay, required!—to bare his soul and exorcise his demons, night in and night out. It was a scenario that simultaneously seduced and frightened him, even before the fans came calling.

Whether they were seeking it or not, fame came calling for Pearl Jam almost immediately. "Alive," the first single from *Ten* and the first song in Vedder's "mamasan trilogy," hit the airwaves in the summer of 1991. Despite the esoteric specificity of the lyrics, it was the perfect choice for a single, as it established Pearl Jam's entire aesthetic in the first eighteen seconds: the big arena-rock riff, the no-nonsense production, the serpentine bass lines, and Vedder's iconic pipes. By the time the optimistic, anthemic chorus kicked in, Pearl Jam had converted legions of fans almost instantaneously.

Though "Alive" was clearly a great song (and to this day remains a defining number in Pearl Jam's catalog and still possibly their most recognizable), it was the video that captured the minds of fans. For a group who would swear off videos later in their career, Pearl Jam owes a lot to their first visual representations. The clip for "Alive" is deceptively simple: Shot in black-and-white, it is little more than a performance video bookended by shots of waves crashing on a shoreline. Looked at today, it seems comically low budget and even a little lazy, but Pearl Jam's performance is electric. The video is probably best remembered for the sequence where Vedder scales the speaker stacks, climbs up to a balcony, hangs like a chimpanzee for a few seconds, and then drops onto the waiting crowd below in an unbearably dangerous stage dive— "Crazy Eddie" at his finest.

Though performance videos are common, the video for "Alive" worked from several different angles to not only establish Pearl Jam as a band but also establish the so-called Seattle sound (or at least the *feel* of the Seattle scene) in one fell swoop. For one thing, the fashion sense was immediately apparent: Vedder wears a flannel shirt, Jeff Ament wears a goofy hat that would become a bit of a trademark, and several band members are wearing shorts. The whole presentation is very casual, which immediately sent the message that this was a group that didn't care about fashion, or at least didn't care about fashion in the traditional rock-and-roll sense (and especially not in the same way that the still-popular metal bands, like Warrant, cared about fashion). The casualness of the clip gave the impression that "Alive" was something like a piece of found footage, which certainly helped with their authenticity. Due to its documentary-like nature, it also lent legitimacy to the crowd reaction—people immediately recognized Pearl Jam as a band that could make an audience go completely apeshit. That may have also worked against their image, however—most people expected Eddie to leap from a balcony *every single time* the band played the song; it probably set up some unreasonable expectations and led to some absurd sense of resentment among fans who wanted to see Vedder cheat death every night.

Even so, Vedder became a guy whom fans gravitated toward. He was a front man who looked like a regular guy, who dressed like a regular guy, and seemed honest and hardworking to a fault. His commitment to his fans seemed almost superhuman, including the daredevil stunts and the fact that he sweat his ass off during performances—something that is very visible in the "Alive" video. Most important, during the *Ten* era he mastered an incredible lyrical niche for himself, where he wrote very personal, vaguely autobiographical songs that sounded like they could be universal. "Alive" is an excellent example—the verse lays out the first chapter of the "mamasan trilogy," where the young man discovers the man he knew as his father was actually an impostor. It's a dense story to tell and sounds like it needs a greater context. It barely rhymes. Then the band arrives at the chorus, where Vedder unleashes the line that made the hook, "I'm still alive." Taken by itself, it sounds like a generic arena-rock refrain, an excuse to close your eyes, light your lighter, and shout along with Eddie. Vedder surfed the line between utterly personal and comically universal with ease, and that was tremendously important. Suddenly, whether you liked confessional, meaningful songs or you just wanted to rock out, you had one guy who could provide both.

This was an important tenet of the reasoning behind grunge's unlikely popularity: its ability to bridge the gap between music fans. Kurt Cobain was certainly the ultimate example of a guy who cared so little about a niche that he managed to attract everybody: Punk-rock kids took Nirvana's roots to heart, metal kids liked that it was loud and melodic, and sensitive types related to Cobain's wails of suffering and aggressive, confessional lyrics. There was something in it for everyone, even though by design it didn't seem like there was anything in it for *anyone*.

Pearl Jam was a similar sort of band. While they didn't display any immediate punk influences outside of the occasional live cover of the Dead Boys' "Sonic Reducer," their easygoing style and shambolic appearance certainly suggested an air of authenticity (something that punk-rock purists tend to value above all else). Metal fans embraced Pearl Jam because they were loud and soloed a lot, and they even attracted a good number of hippies to their cause. That connection wasn't immediately made apparent, though it became more obvious later on when the band collaborated with the likes of Neil Young, Ben Harper, and Jack Johnson, all feel-good roots rockers in their own right. The bottom line was this: You could smoke pot to most Pearl Jam songs and not completely freak out (something that was impossible to do with *Nevermind*). Though one of grunge's legacies is a sense of misanthropy toward fans or would-be admirers, these bands (Pearl Jam especially) bridged gaps without even really trying. Pearl Jam's eclecticism was entirely organic, as their sound was the natural combination of a bunch of metal guys from Seattle and a surfer from San Diego. Pearl Jam never sat down and wondered how they could appeal to more people; much to their chagrin, people just kept hopping onboard.

TEN WAS released on August 27, 1991, via Epic Records, roughly one month before *Nevermind* hit store shelves. The album title was an homage to their former name, as pro basketball player Mookie Blaylock wore the jersey number 10 throughout his NBA career. *Ten* entered the charts relatively quietly but would eventually go on to peak at the number-two position on the Billboard 200 and sell over 10 million copies domestically.

Though they readily admit the album title was merely an homage to their own band name (and thus a tribute to the point guard for the New Jersey Nets), the title represents more levels of Pearl Jam than they had probably intended. When one is considering the band as a construction, with associated imagery and language, rather than just a bunch of guys playing songs, the number 10 transcends several of those layers. First and foremost, *Ten* could easily represent "10" in the Bo Derek sense, as in "perfect 10." If rock-and-roll albums were represented as women, *Ten* would be a well-built supermodel: sexy, striking, enticing, and mysterious. Despite the heavy lyrical content, this was an album that was meant to be populist and to be enjoyed by as many people as possible. Each song is meticulously constructed and was produced with a fine-tooth comb. The pacing is nearly perfect, as the big anthems are offset nicely by ballads—a skill that would later become foreign to the band as their career continued. *Ten* spoke to their need for perfection and precision, and much in the same way that *Appetite for Destruction* is simultaneously carefully scrubbed and magnificently filthy, *Ten* was designed to deliver on both levels: dangerous enough to entice the outcasts, but big and cool enough to bring in the mainstream. Few albums manage to accomplish that, and of all the records that define the grunge era, *Ten* was essentially the only album to actively service both sides of the divide. *Nevermind* certainly brought in a large crossover audience, but that success came from sheer force of will. Kurt Cobain didn't write songs for everybody; he typically wrote songs only for himself. *Ten* was written with no audience in mind, which is why it appealed to everyone.

This sense of perfection, of meticulous machinations to please an audience, doesn't just extend to the title of Pearl Jam's debut. It's quite telling that they originally named themselves after a basketball player, as sports (specifically basketball) have always played a role in the life of the band. Pickup basketball games ruled downtime during their Lollapalooza stint in 1992; during the height of his exposure, Vedder was a fixture at Seattle's Key Arena, where the Supersonics play. It's no wonder that Pearl Jam's debut is rife with hoops imagery: On the front cover, the five band members (making up the same number as the starting lineup on a roundball squad) have their hands clasped together, almost as though they are high-fiving one an other. When the liner notes are unfolded, they reveal a poster that features the band huddled together with their hands raised, as though they have called a time-out and are about to get back into the game with ten seconds to go in need of a stop. It's a pretty complete package with a consistent set of images.

However, the problem with the sports imagery is twofold. First, it completely deviates from the model of grunge as we know it: as a genre of music embraced by outcast culture, co-opted by the mainstream. But what does playing basketball have to do with being an outcast? The kids who wore flannel, grew their hair long, and listened to bands with names like Gruntruck were doing it to get *away* from the guys on the basketball team who taunted them in gym class. What was the draw of music made by those guys? The band members themselves certainly didn't look the part, but they embraced the imagery.

Of course, the disconnect only really reveals itself in hindsight. In the context of the music world circa 1991, hair metal was still holding on to the imaginations of record buyers. Only a year prior, one of metal's most successful and definitive albums had been released in Warrant's *Cherry Pie*. The fact that no member of Pearl Jam resembled Jani Lane and that they weren't making sophomoric videos featuring slices of pie falling into a woman's lap made them the immediate deviants from the mainstream. Pearl Jam hit upon a bizarre chemistry, allowing them to embrace a trope that had long been the domain of the oppressors (like sports) and make it their own. If rock bands were to be believed, the mainstream kids listening to *Cherry Pie* only really cared about getting laid and scoring drugs, which makes the dedicated guy with a weak left hand but a wicked jump shot the outcast by default. Classic cultural tropes, for a brief period, were spun around entirely, which is how Pearl Jam allowed themselves to be gaga over a millionaire point guard and still seem transgressive.

The irony is that it's probable that none of this was conscious, or at least that is what the members of Pearl Jam would prefer you to believe. The band wanted to come across as a group of regular guys, a key attitude in the grunge oeuvre and an important secret to their success. Pearl Jam came across as a band that had constructed nothing at all, and they just happened to like basketball. To a punk-rock kid, sports are wholly uncool (though sometimes if they're extreme, they're okay), but there was a definite lack of pretension in Pearl Jam's admitting that they were hoops fans, and moreso that they were inspired by that set of imagery and into the concept of a "team" (no doubt they perceived themselves as the starting five of a workmanlike squad—probably the Stockton/Malone Utah Jazz). It was obvious they weren't trying to hide anything or form an outsiders identity—they just came entirely as they were. Sometimes that's not necessarily enough to win over the sort of people who consider these things, but in the context of spandex pants and high-heeled boots, it was unbelievably refreshing to see people playing rock songs while looking so aggressively *normal*, and sometimes normalcy is all anybody is really looking for.

WHETHER THEY wanted it or not, the eleven songs Pearl Jam placed on *Ten* became the definitive sonic blueprint for the grunge era. Nirvana may have inspired more wannabes (most notably Bush and Silverchair), but those bands tended to be dismissed as nothing more than what they were (at least by rock critics and other people who think about these kinds of things). Meanwhile, every other band that put an album out between 1992 and 1997 sounded *exactly* like Pearl Jam, and there are still a great number of bands that are making albums that sound like *Ten.* There's no real mystery as to why this is true. In this situation, as in most things in life, the simplest, most logical explanation turns out to be accurate: Pearl Jam was simply easy to copy. Though Kurt Cobain's band borrowed sounds from a number of different sources, Kurt himself was too much of an individual, and his personality was so singular and complicated that it was far too difficult to construct a reasonable doppelgänger that produced the same sort of attitude. In Pearl Jam's case, the "regular guys" stance made them pretty universal—if you had a couple of arena-size riffs, a ballad about abuse, and a brooding baritone for a front man, you had yourself a platinum rock band.

This may sound like an insult to Pearl Jam—that their sound was so simple (and thus uncomplicated) that anybody could make it big by parroting them. While this may be true, it shouldn't be construed as a slight—universality is much more difficult than singularity. There's nothing terribly hard about being an individual. Generally, all it takes is a slightly insane worldview and the right combination of drugs. Appealing to large numbers of people but still seeming so accessible that other people can actually replicate your individual and band personalities takes a very delicate chemistry, and Pearl Jam did it without even trying. After all, the best things are often universal, and universal things are easily replicated. Nobody argues that Led Zeppelin is not the greatest hard-rock band in history (except for a couple of misguided King Crimson fans), and that's because (1) their songs sounded simple and because of that (2) everybody *could* love them. A lot of people refer to Metallica as the next-generation Led Zeppelin, but when broken down, Pearl Jam looks to fit the bill a little better.

Ten is one of those incredible albums that sound absolutely effortless, and if reports are to be believed, it mostly was. So inspired by each other were Pearl Jam that *Ten* was ground out in only in a matter of weeks in what has got to be an absolutely unprecedented surge of creativity and energy. The sonic casualness of their debut helps immensely, as songs that would normally sound overwrought (such as "Garden") are given a buoyancy that only a tremendous amount of comfort and trust among band members can provide.

The album opens with a driving, surging guitar line that after a few seconds gives way to the bass and drums and becomes the groove of "Once." A prototypical album opener, "Once" perfectly introduces Pearl Jam's aesthetic: groovy, jittery arena-rock riffs, an intense storytelling quality to the verses, a bridge you could chant along to, and a huge chorus. With all that in place, though, the secret to "Once" is in its lyrics. As the second act of the mamasan trilogy, it tells the story of how the young boy from "Alive" goes off the deep end and commits horrible acts of violence that are completely beyond him. He bemoans the negative trajectory of his personal evolution. As always, the most important lyric is in the chorus: "Once upon a time I could control myself."

For obvious reasons, those lyrics are a problem, mostly because they tell the second part of a story that nobody was even aware of in the first place. For somebody who simply put on *Ten*, "Once" is entirely without context, which renders the narrative strength of the song completely useless. However, this might have inadvertently played to Pearl Jam's advantage, as the lyrics to "Once" can be rendered completely meaningless and still be important.

Rock lyrics are overrated. Though they're often analyzed as poetry and looked upon as the vessel for whatever the "message" of a song is, there are maybe a half-dozen lyricists in rock history who actually had something to say. Mostly lyrics only have to *sound* good, in the sense that the sounds or meanings of the individual words complement the music in an appropriate manner. For most of the rock community, as long as the lyrics sound cool, it hardly matters what is being talked about. Though there's no doubt that James Hetfield would claim his lyrics are important, the line "Darkness imprisoning me" only works because it is absolutely the most logical line to match with the riff from "One." Who cares what it's about as long as it sounds absolutely transcendent when chanted by twenty thousand people at an arena?

"Once" works the same way. There is a story behind the song, but more important, "Once upon a time I could control myself" is exactly the kind of line that teenagers want to scream at the top of their lungs when the chorus hits. Though he didn't embrace the concept (at least not at this point in his career), Eddie Vedder's songs won over fans and inspired legions of followers because his songs could be rendered completely meaningless. Obviously they had meaning to him, but an amazing bit of chemistry somehow managed to occur: When he made his lyrics very specific, they became almost entirely universal. Look at the second track on *Ten*, "Even Flow." One of Pearl Jam's biggest all-time singles and still a live staple (it's the one song that appears on almost every single live bootleg the band has released), "Even Flow" is ostensibly about a homeless guy named Even. Songs immortalizing the imagination and industry of the homeless rarely top the charts, but the secret was in the somewhat nonsensical chorus, which had lines like "Thoughts arrive like butterflies." Live performances of the song reveal its two secrets. First, it's amazingly fun to sing, and though outside of the context of the song the lyrics sound unbearably silly (and even sound sort of ridiculous *within* the context), it sounds awesome. Therein lies the second secret: Vedder is committed to the lyrics, and he is mostly committed to the lyrics sounding cool. Nobody was able to sell a nonsense lyric like Eddie Vedder—not even the guy who rhymed the word "mosquito" with "libido." Granted,

Cobain's lyrics might have actually been nonsense, but Vedder took extremely personal lyrics and made them sound completely meaningless, which is the best way to make them sound great. Again, this may seem like a bit of a backhanded compliment, but if Pearl Jam had embraced what they were already doing–allowing for things to be universal and not taking themselves so seriously–they might not have run into the problems they ran into later in their long and rocky career.

WITH *TEN* on the books and tearing up the charts, Pearl Jam continued to ride the wave of success that they first saw with "Alive." A similar video for "Even Flow" followed suit, but when it came time to release "Jeremy" as a single in mid-1992, the band wanted to do something completely different. They hired Mark Pellington, a relatively unknown video director who would later helm high-profile clips for U2, Nine Inch Nails, and Foo Fighters (like many video directors, he later graduated to features, directing the underrated terrorism thriller *Arlington Road* in 1999 and 2002's *The Mothman Prophecies*, one of the least watchable films of the new century). The video, which became not only one of the defining pieces of imagery for the grunge era but also one of the definitive pieces of culture for an entire generation, shot Pearl Jam to the pop culture forefront and became a lightning rod for controversy.

"Jeremy" was a fairly unusual song in the context of *Ten*. Recorded late in the production process, it came together when Eddie Vedder read the true story of a sixteen-year-old kid named Jeremy Wade Delle, who took his own life in front of his classmates in January of 1991. Though Pearl Jam would later write copious tunes based on other people's stories or current events, "Jeremy" was an early experiment for Vedder and the band. The song opens with the now-familiar bass riff and some very unusual guitar tones, as though the notes are being banged around with a tack hammer. Once the drums enter, Vedder's heavy baritone narrates a story about a kid who draws violent pictures and gets ignored by his parents. The chorus, featuring gospel-tinged backing vocals, contains one haunting line: "Jeremy spoke in class today." It's an odd little tune that happens to be catchy as hell and became a huge hit.

Pellington's video is so literal that it could almost be called artless. It depicts a young boy alone in the woods, drawing and posing in various pained tableaux. He is also shown in a school uniform being mocked by other kids. The song ends with an impressive and haunting image: the schoolroom full of kids, frozen in place, covered in Jeremy's blood. The standards and practices department of MTV prevented Pellington and Pearl Jam from including what would have been the money shot: the actual footage of Jeremy putting a gun in his mouth. Instead, all that's shown is the reaction from the class.

When "Jeremy" premiered on MTV, it became an instant sensation and almost immediately thereafter became hugely controversial. Without the image of the young boy turning the gun on himself, many people thought that the final image of the video suggested that Jeremy had opened fire on his classmates (a suggestion that foreshadowed the rash of school shootings that gripped the United States several years later). The song was interpreted as a revenge fantasy, and Pearl Jam came under fire for advocating violence. Vedder was forced to defend his band, his song, and his video at every turn—is it any wonder that the band started to shy away from the spotlight and vowed to never again make a video after this incident?

The "Jeremy" fiasco and Pearl Jam's subsequent process of "scaling back" bring up one of the key sticking points about grunge that never quite felt right: the idea of shunning fame. Eddie

Vedder (along with Cobain and countless others) talked repeatedly about not wanting to be famous, and most of the bands carried themselves with a similar attitude. Cynics would wonder why the bands would even bother releasing albums or calling attention to themselves with videos if they didn't want to be famous, but it's not quite as simple as that. For a while (and this is a key piece of the puzzle that adds up to what grunge truly meant to rock and roll), these guys were able to live the artist's dream—they were able to make what they wanted, and it was commercially successful. They were able to enjoy the benefits of selling out without actually selling out. They were told that there was nothing else like them happening and that they could make music that was noncommercial and meaningful and still make a living out of it, and this made them the most dangerous people in the universe.

People always complain that the best musicians never get the sort of fame they deserve (Stephen Malkmus is often mentioned in this conversation). But history has taught us that the bands that had their cake and ate it, too (which is a very short list), stopped making quality records in the end. They got caught up in their own meaning, so much so that they completely ignored whatever it was that made them good in the first place. But they'll sacrifice innovation for the sake of becoming something more—this is a realization that Bono stumbled upon after the *Pop* debacle. Bono realized that rather than become a postirony art project, if U2 kept writing the same songs they had written since the eighties they could *mean* something and bands that mean something don't have to worry about being good. The music becomes beside the point, secondary to the greater construction of "the band." For fans, liking U2 has almost nothing to do with whether or not you enjoy the songs on *All That You Can't Leave Behind* and has everything to do with whether or not you are willing to align yourself with Bono's politics.

This is why "Jeremy" (both the song and the video) is problematic. On the one hand, it's an incredibly catchy song that is loud, sounds good in arenas, and inspires sing-alongs. But on the other hand, it tells a current-events story and the video attempts to take a stand on teenage suicide. So the song is both ass-kicking cool and "important" in some way. This type of combination does not compute. Rock fans need their big stars to be stupid and empty because they don't want to have to process something that's supposed to be fun, and they need their smart, meaningful rockers to be difficult and misunderstood. That became Pearl Jam's problem: "Smart" rock fans and "dumb" rock fans both liked them equally, and those two groups do not get along. "Smart" rock fans need their music to be strange and esoteric (this is most often expressed by listening to Tool), and "dumb" rock fans just want something to sing along to while they drive home from work. Depending on which side of the fence you stood on, Pearl Jam either made smart rock too dumb or dumb rock too "thinky," and therein was their downfall.

But of course there's no such thing as bad publicity. With the success of the "Jeremy" single and video, *Ten* continued to sell, and now that the "Jeremy" video had been covered by news outlets that wouldn't normally cover rock bands, Pearl Jam became a household name. In raising their own profile, they also raised the profile of their Seattle brethren—all of a sudden, everybody was going back to do their grunge story a second time. "Smells Like Teen Spirit" was the first push, and "Jeremy" provided the second push. It had transcended the concept of a fluke—grunge had arrived on the mainstream's doorstep, and there it would stay (for a couple of years, anyway).

Whether they intended to or not, Pearl Jam reaped the most immediate benefits of the continued surge of grunge's popularity—a surge they helped to directly create. The frenzy over their sophomore album was one that hadn't been seen since *Use Your Illusion* was making its way to store shelves. At the 1993 MTV Video Music Awards (the same ceremony that showered Pearl Jam with moon men for the "Jeremy" clip), Pearl Jam backed Neil Young in a stirring rendition of "Rockin' in the Free World," giving them a weight and importance that no other grunge band had received so publicly. They were being acknowledged by the old guard as a force in rock and roll. Later that night, Pearl Jam performed "Animal," a brand-new song that would appear on their new album, a performance that has gone down in history as not only one of the most energetic and passionate in the history of the VMAs but also one of the only performances on the show of a song that was never attached to a video (though it was released as a single, Pearl Jam had vowed to never again make videos after "Jeremy," a practice they upheld until "Do the Evolution" in 1998). When *Vs.* was finally released a month later, it set an all-time record for copies sold in the first week of release, moving 950,000 units, a record the band held for five years until it was broken by N*SYNC (though technically Pearl Jam still owned the record, as Soundscan had changed their reporting system from five days to seven days since the release of *Vs.*, so N*SYNC's number represented two extra days of sales).

But right when it looked like Pearl Jam was on top of the world, things began to crumble. The week after *Vs.* set the sales record, Vedder was featured on the cover of *Time* magazine and discussed in an article that attempted to sum up the entire alternative rock scene in one piece, dragging everybody from Pearl Jam and Nirvana to Babes in Toyland and Soul Asylum into the tent. Admittedly, it's a thankless job trying to extract the meaning of the grunge movement in one thirty-five-hundred-word magazine article (this book is over twenty times that length and *still* doesn't do a very good job of that), but it brought to the mainstream a lot of the issues that had until then gone mostly unspoken in the grunge communtiy. Suddenly everybody's dirty laundry (mostly having to do with Vedder's rejection of fame) was out in the open. A large chunk of the article was devoted to how many grunge rockers (including Stone Temple Pilots' Scott Weiland) were uncomfortable about the fact that their music attracted the same young guys who beat them up in high school.

But the article did bring up the idea that is at its core not only the most problematic aspect of Pearl Jam's success but also the most troubling question of the alternative-rock era: If grunge is meant to be a rejection of the mainstream, but then it becomes the mainstream, what is it the "alternative" to? Kurt Cobain realized the potential for hypocrisy in such a concept, which is partially why he made *In Utero* consciously uncommercial. But Pearl Jam essentially stuck to their guns on *Vs.*, and though there were several esoteric experiments (most notably the atmospheric "W.M.A." and the somewhat goofy funk romp "Rats"), *Vs.* became huge on the backs of rousing rockers such as "Animal," "Daughter," and "Glorified G," along with the soulful ballads that Pearl Jam had perfected (most notably in the hauntingly beautiful "Elderly Woman Behind the Counter in a Small Town"). Just as it was with their first record, they made an album that could easily be described as arena rock, and just like *Ten* (which was still in the Billboard Top 30 when *Vs.* debuted), it sold millions of copies and hung around in the upper echelons of the charts for months. In a way, Vedder and Pearl Jam walked away with more integrity than Cobain, because while Kurt took evasive action in order to avoid being labeled a hypocrite, it didn't matter to Pearl Jam that they were being called hypocrites. Just as they had done in Mother Love Bone, the Pearl Jam guys wanted to be rock stars, and they had done just that.

Of course, Eddie's earnest leanings complicated the scenario, but he spent a decade going out of his way to prove that he meant everything all along: He tried to take on Ticketmaster in an antitrust case; he's worked with environmental charities and stumped politically for John Kerry and Ralph Nader. Of course, these are the very things that make Vedder tremendously easy to hate. But in reality, Eddie Vedder might be the least hypocritical front man since Gene Simmons. With Gene, you always knew his motives and you always knew what you were getting (typically "he wanted to bone you" and "you were going to get boned"). Eddie's causes have regularly been more noble. Even though they haven't made an exceptional album since 1994's *Vitalogy*, Pearl Jam has remained the largest group still standing from the grunge era, and they are still able to sell out just about any venue they play. Love them or hate them, they remain one of the most important musical groups of the twentieth century. Of course, sometimes it's better to just be good than it is to be important, but Pearl Jam took on the mantle of being an "important band," and as with U2 and R.E.M. before them, their fans have mostly stuck with them with questionable musical experiments and bizarre associations. Sometimes it pays to be this earnest.

CHAPTER 6

—

HEROIN

A Bad Idea Comes to Town

THE MANTRA GOES "SEX, DRUGS, AND ROCK 'N' ROLL," AND FIT-
tingly, every new rock movement always has a specific drug that
tends to color it. Whatever it is, it tends to be enjoyed by both the
musicians in order to create the music with ease and the fans in order to make the terrible drug-influenced music more palatable.
For every musical revolution there is a similar narcotic revolution.
Oddly, there never appears to be a definitive movement for the
"sex" portion of "sex, drugs, and rock 'n' roll," though one could
easily deduce that glam metal's defining position would be up
against the wall of a strip club. Hip-hop varies, but it's always from
behind. Grunge? Straight missionary, though failing that, rigorous,
semidepressing masturbation.

But getting back on-topic, the relationship between music, especially rock music, and drugs cannot be understated. Drugs will absolutely define a band's total aesthetic, from the way the songs
sound, to what their T-shirts should say, to what their groupies will
look like, to how the band members will eventually die. For example, look at a band that existed at the same time as the grunge
movement but had nothing to do with it whatsoever: Phish.

Carrying the torch for the Grateful Dead in the sense that thousands of nonshowering people followed them around from place to place wasting the money in their trust funds, Phish attracted totalitarian pot use and casual experiments with hallucinogens. Though the band's music initially established the drug aesthetic, the drugs inevitably came back around to influence the band (i.e., there were initially surreal lyrics in Phish songs, but as the use of mushrooms at their shows escalated, so did the surrealism in the lyrics). The rest of the group's details fell into place: The T-shirts had to be trippy but not so trippy that they would cause a freak-out, the band dressed like college students, and the women who followed them all had dreadlocks and wore ankle-length hemp skirts. Had Phish stayed together, you can bet one of them would have eventually drowned in a vat of Chunky Monkey while on a particularly gnarly trip.

Grunge's precursor, glam metal, also had a very intimate relationship with drugs, though it's a little trickier to define. The knee-jerk reaction would seemingly be obvious: Those bands seemed to be on a never-ending binge on cocaine. That's not to say that there weren't other narcotics being passed around (in *The Dirt*, the members of Mötley Crüe extoll the virtues of "zombie dust," which is a mixture of cocaine and sedative called Halcyon that sounds unbelieveably dangerous). In a socioeconomic context, cocaine was also the defining drug of the eighties (it was expensive and seemed glamorous, especially to people watching *Dallas*), but it's that glamour that kept it from really being the chemical that brought band and audience together. The people listening to metal weren't glamorous; as *American Psycho* illustrates, the regular people who were actually doing cocaine in the eighties were more concerned with Huey Lewis than Cinderella. The metal crowd was working class, and as many terrible metal videos pointed out, a lot of that crowd were living out their fantasies through the music. While it wasn't too hard to live like your favorite group if you were a Phish fan, it was nearly impossible to even fathom living the same lifestyle as your favorite metal band (especially if your favorite band was Kiss). Plus, there was a level of impracticality in even obtaining cocaine. Unless you lived in or near a major coastal city, coke wasn't something that was easy to come by, and as metal was always more popular in the Midwest than anywhere else, that threw up another barrier. The closest metal fans were able to get to their idols, at least on a chemical level, was through alcohol. The defining liquor was probably whiskey (mostly because of the famed L.A. club of the same name and Slash's affinity for Jack Daniel's, but any hooch would do. When broken down, it made perfect sense: Metal riffs are based on power chords, which are in turn blues based, and the blues has always been drinking music. Though most of the bands were on it, cocaine didn't necessarily make metal better—in fact, considering coke's effect on the central nervous system, it's bound to make a lot of metal songs sound infinitely worse. Coke makes catchy music sound lame and terrible music sound transcendent; this is why Interpol is a coke band.

When grunge came along, it brought with it a drug that was arguably making its mainstream debut: heroin. Of course, grunge bands weren't the first groups to realize the importance of heroin. In fact, the coolest people in the history of music all dabbled in horse at one time or another: Keith Richards, Miles Davis, Jimi Hendrix—the list goes on. But grunge bands were the first to be using heroin as a collective, and since the music's patron saint had a well-documented problem with the drug, that brought it into the zeitgeist for the first time, in the sense that suddenly everybody's mom knew what heroin was, how it affected the central nervous system, and what the best methods of tying off were. But using the preceding logic regarding metal, heroin would seemingly be disqualified as the representative chemical of the grunge era because the audience, in general, was not using it. Heroin use certainly went up in the beginning of the nineties, but that trend had already been building well before the grunge era identified with the drug. Still, heroin defined grunge's aesthetic so thoroughly and completely that it cannot be denied, especially considering the social ramifications of heroin use and the music itself.

HEROIN IS an opiate derived of morphine, which is synthesized from the seedpods of several different poppies. It was first developed in 1874 and was manufactured and distributed as a pain reliever and cough medicine. In fact, Bayer (who had already developed a patent for an analgesic called aspirin) trademarked the name Heroin in 1898 and sold it in liquid form until 1910. The name was a derivative of the German word *heroisch*, which loosely translated to "heroic" in English. By 1914, the U.S. government realized heroin's addictive properties and it became illegal to manufacture, sell, or own heroin in the United States. From that point on, most of the world's heroin came from Turkey, but pressure from the United States in the 1960s forced the Turks to shut down poppy production. Most of the world's heroin is now drawn from Mexico, Colombia, Afghanistan, and the "Golden Triangle," which straddles Laos, Vietnam, Thailand, and Myanmar.

Modern heroin is sold in bags of white or brown powder. While logic would dictate that the brown powder would be the more impure, the color actually depends on the type of poppies used; in actuality, it was far more common for white heroin to contain contaminants, as it could be cut with anything from baking powder to battery acid. Brown heroin is mostly cut with innocuous brown sugar. These impurities were so universal that the process of cooking heroin up and injecting it directly into the veins was a necessity.

Today, however, most of the heroin that comes into the United States is much cheaper than it used to be and thus is less likely to be cut with anything dangerous, and so it is safe enough to snort.

The effects of heroin are well documented. While small doses offer the thorough pain relief of morphine, a large injection will result in a rapid interaction with the nerve receptors in the brain, resulting in a state of euphoria that can last up to six hours. As it is described in Irvine Welsh's *Trainspotting* (perhaps the ultimate heroin text), "Take the best orgasm you've ever had, multiply it by a thousand, and you're still nowhere near it."

So what made this drug so popular among the Pacific Northwest rockers of the early nineties? Or rather, more important, why was heroin the definitive grunge drug?

It sounds clichéd, but there is a certain amount of practical logic to heroin being popular in Seattle. It just makes sense that Seattlelites would be drawn to a depressant, as the city is relatively isolated and receives two hundred days of cloud covering per year. Conditions such as those are quite conducive to depression, and if grunge had one particular stock-in-trade, it was depression. In the music and in the attitude, depression informed grunge. While the metallers of the eighties were just looking for a good time, both grunge rockers and grunge fans were brooding. Of course, that's not to say that all grunge bands were singing about the issues they had with their parents, like Eddie Vedder or Kurt Cobain. In fact, some of the most important bands seemed pretty well-adjusted: Mudhoney sang about being sick, but it always seemed like they just drank too much; Screaming Trees sang psychedelic love songs (though front man Mark Lanegan's solo albums are now nothing but brooding); all of Andrew Wood's most important songs seemed to be about slaying mythical beasts. Contrary to popular belief, the scene was not all moping all the time.

However, it's important to remember that popular belief will be how the general populace will be informed of the scene as time passes. As far as history is concerned, all grunge rockers *were* depressed and everybody wore nothing but flannel all the time. These are certainly fallacies, but they are close enough to the general truth to be considered fact, and thus that is how they will be processed, and as we move further and further away from that era, these half-truths will become more and more absolute. The musicians themselves can resist and protest all they want, but this process is inevitable and has already been in motion for years.

That's what makes heroin such an interesting phenomenon in the context of the grunge movement. As far as that general collective history is concerned, everybody was on heroin all the time and that informed everything about the scene. Ironically, heroin didn't really cement itself as a prominent drug until much later; when grunge bands were first getting their feet wet (in the *Deep Six* era), the drug of choice was, remarkably, MDA.

"MDA" stands for "methyldioxyamphetamine" and is today associated more with the rave scene. Its effects are consistent with that culture: heightened senses, energy surges, and mild hallucinations. "There was a time when it seemed like everybody was on MDA," says Mark Arm. The drug was a staple of Green River and early Mudhoney shows and, according to Arm, helped foster a feeling of brotherhood among the bands in the scene (even though it was more or less an artificial feeling). So even though MDA informed some of the most seminal moments in grunge history, nobody ever seems to bring it up. It's a logical dismissal considering that on a purely superficial level the drug has next to nothing to do with the way the music sounds and the way the musicians carried themselves. There have never been any great writers who took club drugs to try to be more creative–when they wanted the award-winning ideas to flow, they turned to the needle.

Of course, this leads to another one of heroin's supposed draws: creativity. There is a romantic suggestion that people who use heroin experience a freedom of ideas and that the drug will make them more creative and more prolific with artistic endeavors. Writers seem to have cornered the market on this concept, with William S. Burroughs and Hunter Thompson leading the charge and achieving great success in the process. Musicians have been no strangers to the white lady, either, as icons Miles Davis and Keith Richards both found themselves under the spell at points in their careers (and both used the drug not only for recreation but for writing assistance as well).

Like most of the aspects of grunge that eventually became broad clichés, it started with Cobain. Ironically, Kurt started using heroin as a way to combat a debilitating stomach problem that had plagued him most of his life. There was rarely a time when Cobain wasn't nauseous, and he vomited constantly. According to Michael Azerrad's biography, *Come as You Are: The Story of Nirvana*, the ailment was caused by Cobain's spine rubbing up against his stomach. Kurt was diagnosed with a mild form of scoliosis, which is a curvature of the spine that can be easily corrected by wearing a brace in childhood. Kurt's spine curved out a bit on his right side, but it was made worse by the fact that he played guitar left-handed (and thus held his guitar with his right shoulder). Ironically, Cobain was naturally right-handed, and it's been theorized that had he played guitar that way, the spinal curvuture may have corrected itself over time.

It's hard to tell how much heroin might have affected Kurt's songwriting. "Something in the Way" certainly has the foggy, watery feeling of a heroin high, and Kurt's guttural yelping always sounded like he was coming down off a bad buzz. But whether he was intending to or not, nothing Kurt wrote ever held a candle to the definitive heroin album by the definitive heroin band: *Dirt*, the 1992 magnum opus by Alice in Chains.

Layne Staley grew up in the Seattle suburbs and started a glam metal band while he was still in high school. He called his band Alice N Chainz. In 1987, he met songwriter and guitarist Jerry Cantrell, who suggested the band be called Alice in Chains and who brought along a heavier metal edge to the proceedings. Staley was obsessed with S&M and gender reversal, which is why the band name has an S&M overtone and their earliest gigs were played in drag. Cantrell's friends Mike Starr and Sean Kinney rounded out the line-up, and by 1989 the band had signed to Columbia Records.

Their debut EP, *We Die Young*, became a moderate hit when the title track made waves on rock radio. Their 1990 debut full-length, *Facelift*, followed close behind, and the breakout smash "Man in the Box" helped earn them an opening spot on a Van Halen tour and propelled *Facelift* to Gold status.

Facelift is a loud, brutal, and punishing hour of rock, heavily steeped in the dirgey, blues-based metal of Black Sabbath, Deep Purple, and Motorhead. "Man in the Box" is a relentless guitar-led death march, and it also introduced the world to Staley's singing voice, which in its upper registers sounds like he is being exorcised of demons (this wail is also best heard on the song "Sludge Factory," from AIC's self-titled 1995 album). It's a voice full of pain, paranoia, and desperation—customized for Alice in Chains' sound.

As a follow-up to their successful debut, Alice in Chains put out a fascinating EP called *Sap*. At first glance it just seemed like a batch of leftovers from the *Facelift* sessions put out as a stopgap between full-lengths, but on *Sap* four acoustic ballads actually revealed the melancholy side of Alice in Chains. "Got Me Wrong" became a hit, and the expectations rose for the band's next proper album.

In the fall of 1992, Alice in Chains released *Dirt*, one of the best albums of the grunge era. Staley had already been in the throes of addiction for years by the time the band got around to writing the songs for this album, and even though not every song is about heroin (notably Cantrell's tribute to his Vietnam-vet father, "Rooster"), the struggles of Staley's addiction are all over the lyrics, and he seems constantly overwhelmed. The album opens with Staley yelping at the top of "Them Bones," a pounding juggernaut of an opening track. Cantrell's waves of guitar gunk threaten to overwhelm Staley, who sounds like he's trying to outrun his own shadow. But in the end, he admits that he'll be nothing but dust soon.

Staley spends the rest of the album bemoaning his own fate, admitting that he has lost control and that there's no hope for him. Heroin is a difficult drug to kick—by many accounts, even junkies who have cleaned up still have to deal with "the hunger"—and Staley gave his own addiction a personality. If you didn't know any better, you could easily infer that Staley is singing about an overdemanding woman. But when he sings "I give this part of me for you" on "Down in a Hole," his only mistress is the needle.

But just because Staley had an intense addiction doesn't automatically make *Dirt* the best heroin album of the era. Plenty of front men have been high and have sung about their addiction (the most confusing of which was Brad Nowell, front man of Sublime, who made pot records). But Alice in Chains and Staley in particular were able to sound exactly what heroin addiction is supposed to sound like: dark, desperate, and ethereal, but with flashes of bliss at the same time. Alice in Chains lived at more extremes than most grunge bands (and certainly more than most heavy metal bands), as they created feedback-heavy fright fests such as "Junkhead" but were also capable of dreaming up beautiful ballads such as "Brother" (from the *Sap* EP). Though it was always dark, Alice in Chains recognized that darkness always felt different, just as the process of heroin addiction has its ups and downs.

Like any great songwriter, Staley was able to express the full range of his inner life while still maintaining an underlying aesthetic. The only other guy who could switch from doom, to bliss, to melancholy and back as well as Staley did was Kurt.

Alice in Chains followed up *Dirt* with an exceptional mini-album called *Jar of Flies* that was similar to *Sap* in that it was a quieter, more reflective group of songs. It ended up being an ideal companion to *Dirt*. While Staley bellowed the songs from *Dirt* from the perspective of a junkie who had closed himself off from the world, the songs from *Jar of Flies* come from the junkie who has realized what his addiction has done to the world around him. Several songs even hint at a desire for self-improvement: On "I Stay Away" Staley thinks about "traveling south this year," while on "No Excuses" he admits: "No more hiding or disguising truths I've sold." Staley always ended up admitting his own doom, but it seemed like some light was beginning to show through.

Of course, it was just the beauty of the songs playing tricks, because in reality, Staley was a mess. It's actually a miracle that Alice in Chains managed to release anything after *Dirt*, as Staley's addiction constantly worsened and he became more and more isolated from his family, friends, and bandmates. Like most junkies, he became more and more unreliable, and Alice in Chains eventually stopped touring, which only fueled the fires of speculation about just how bad Staley was. They did manage to put together one more full-length album in 1995, and they appeared on *MTV Unplugged* in 1996. Though the performance was incredible, Staley's health was clearly fading. In fact, his death was mistakenly reported so often that it became something of an urban legend. The legend was finally put to rest on April 20, 2002, when Staley was found dead of an overdose of heroin and cocaine. Layne Staley spent his career challenging his demons, but the demons ended up with the upper hand.

–

THOUGH IT'S not entirely accurate, heroin will always be the drug that people think about when they think about grunge. It claimed the lives of Andrew Wood and Layne Staley and complicated the lives of Kurt Cobain and Courtney Love. It's been fetishized and obsessed over and will probably always remain a tempting experiment for adventurous songwriters who want to tap into the supposed "enlightening" qualities it possesses. Though heroin use certainly didn't define all of the music from the early nineties, it certainly helped define a specific culture. Anthropologically speaking, heroin seemed designed for grunge-era twentysomethings (or at least the stereotype of grunge-era twentysomethings, which is what people will actually remember): arty, mildly depressed slackers who already did a lot of navel contemplation and listened to turgid rock music. Of course, as stated earlier, this is a stereotype, but that's the problem with rock culture–the history is written mostly by the people who can't remember it very well. Not all new wave looked and sounded like Culture Club, but their specific aesthetic and set of images are what survive, and so they define the genre, rather than the other way aroud. The same goes for hair metal–not everybody looked and sounded like Poison (just look at Tesla), but the glam metal association is a bunch of girlie-looking guys with big hair and tight spandex pants.

So while not every grunge band looked, sounded, and acted like Alice in Chains, they represent a definitive definition of a grunge band. Hardly the most successful (either commercially or critically), Alice in Chains will stand as the definition of what grunge is because they embody the clichés so well. That is why heroin will always be considered the grunge drug.

CHAPTER 7

GRUNGE ON FILM

Angst and Heartbreak with an Amazing Sound Track

IN THE SAME WAY THAT SEVENTIES DISCO HAD *SATURDAY Night Fever* and out-of-control 1980s capitalism had *Wall Street*, the grunge explosion of the early 1990s was a cultural movement that was well represented on film during its heyday. Films that try to capture those kinds of movements as they are happening are fascinating because they do not yet have the benefit of hindsight when considering what's important and what isn't. A lot of the time, the same movies don't contain any aesthetic distance, either, as they are typically made because (1) they are passion projects of people who live and breathe the scene or (2) they are corporate cash-ins that attempt to repackage aspects of culture and then sell it back to the people who had those same concepts stolen from them in the first place. In either instance, a lot of attention is paid to the details (the way people dress, the speech patterns), but little time is given to what the greater message might be (like why people dress and talk the way they do).

Still, with all the problems inherent to such undertakings, there is still no greater window into the heart of a movement than a film that was made when the movement was at its peak. The in-era movie that gives us the earliest lens by which to analyze grunge and the generation that gave the movement life is Cameron Crowe's 1992 opus, *Singles.*

Singles has led an exceptionally strange life as a film. Writer-director Cameron Crowe was already working on the script when Andrew Wood overdosed in 1990. The film was made as a sort of tribute to him. On the surface, *Singles* is a fairly generic romantic comedy that happens to take place in Seattle and happens to star members of Pearl Jam, Soundgarden, and Alice in Chains. At the time it seemed as though it was meant to be one of those corporate cash-ins, though Crowe had the concept for this script as far back as 1984. That the "Seattle sound" happened to explode in between the time *Singles* was shot and the time it was eventually released was simply a happy accident for Warner Bros., who distributed the film.

Singles was not a hit. Estimates have it grossing only $18 million domestically, even though the bands making appearances in the film and on the sound track were the biggest in the land at the time. So much for synergy.

But *Singles* has also gone through a strange evolution. Naturally, considering the popularity of Pearl Jam and Soundgarden at the time, the movie was seen as a youth culture film aimed at the same crowd who would make Alice in Chains' *Dirt* a massive hit only weeks after the film's release. On the surface, it's a forgettable distraction (not unlike most of the hit songs of that era), but underneath, there is way more going on than anybody, including Crowe, could have intended. In the pantheon of Cameron Crowe's work, it's rarely considered among his greater achievements like *Jerry Maguire* (a more traditional romantic comedy) or *Almost Famous* (a purer rock movie). Despite the presence of the bands, it hasn't even gained a cult following—the only DVD version that exists is a single-disc edition with very little in the way of special features, the greatest current measuring stick for a film's popularity or cult status.

Though it was absorbed as a teenage angst film and remembered as a romantic comedy that happened to be dressed in flannel, over time *Singles* has become the most definitive statement on both the bands included in the grunge scene and the people who were consuming and processing that music (and that lifestyle) circa 1992.

Set in a vaguely fictionalized Seattle, *Singles* tells the story of a group of twenty-somethings living a series of vaguely interconnected lives. Steve, played by Campbell Scott, is a guy obsessed with developing a public transit system who meets Linda (Kyra Sedgwick), an environmentalist. Also living in Steve's apartment complex is his ex-girlfriend, Janet (Bridget Fonda), who is the sorta girlfriend of rocker Cliff (Matt Dillon), who fronts a band called Citizen Dick (the other three members of Citizen Dick are Jeff Ament, Stone Gossard, and Eddie Vedder of Pearl Jam). Also in this mix are Bailey (Jim True-Frost), Steve's best friend, who disappears for most of the second half of the film, and Debbie Hunt (Sheila Kelley), a comic-relief man-hunting advertising executive who appears to be lifted from another film entirely (her fashion, speech patterns, and attitudes seem so anachronistic she can pretty much be ignored in this analysis). The main story line belongs to Steve and Linda, though the other characters float in and out. The story is the old boy meets girl, boy loses girl, boy gets girl back, boy panics, and all live happily ever after in the end. In between all this, everybody seems to hang at the same two or three rock clubs where they watch Soundgarden, Pearl Jam, and Alice in Chains perform to crowds of maybe a few hundred.

In truth, *Singles* was a movie that was about young people listening to loud music but became a film about what it was like to be in your twenties at the beginning of the nineties and said more about the state of mind of those people than any other film since. In the midst of all the narrative movement, a lot of things happen along the way that seem minor or inconsequential but actually turn out to be the most important aspects of the film. If Cameron Crowe somehow knew that these things would be as telling as they were to audiences down the line, his level of genius would be absolutely dangerous and he should probably be imprisoned and used for science experiments. Likely, these details made it into the film just because Crowe liked them or they were simply cultural references and tics that seemed aggressively normal at the time. The direct references to grunge are readily apparent: One of Cliff's band's songs is called "Touch Me I'm Dick," which is similar to Mudhoney's "Touch Me I'm Sick." Dillon's character also makes multiple references to the fact that Citizen Dick is beloved in Europe, something that was true of Mudhoney, Tad, and a handful of other protogrunge groups. These copious minor details don't necessarily reflect anything relevant to the film but do reflect the zeitgeist of the times.

The character constructions are very interesting and telling of a certain mentality that permeated the nation's youth and drove them to listen to this loud, depressing music in the first place (in one of the movie's most unintentionally hilarious scenes, Linda talks to one of her friends about when they go out "dancing" and it cuts to the two of them shaking their tail feathers at a club to Pearl Jam's "State of Love and Trust," a song with a truly depressing lyric sheet, then again it *does* have a great beat). Just like in *St. Elmo's Fire*, most of the characters are approaching adulthood and suffering from delusions of grandeur in some form. As stated earlier, Steve is obsessed with traffic patterns and wants to introduce a "Super Train" into Seattle that will provide public transit with music and coffee. Linda wants to save the environment from oil spills (or preserve sea life or protect Alaska—it's never really made clear, actually). Janet wants to go to architecture school. Cliff dreams of rock stardom, which ironically is the most grounded aspiration in this context—in 1992, you'd be way more likely to sign a major-label deal for your Seattle band than to boost mass transit. They all dream very big, some more impractically than others, but more important they want to make other people's lives better. Naturally, sociologists will look back on this phenomenon and deduce that these young people were bucking the trends of the time they were raised (that being the go-go supercapitalist eighties) and will be absolutely right. But rather than just reject their parents' ideals, Steve and Linda take on a mission of (theoretically) greater good, and it becomes their burden. Steve repeatedly says that he uses work as an escape, and that particular sentiment permeated the landscape of youth in the early nineties (no matter what anybody says, the "slacker" concept never really fit these people well— remember that only half a decade later they were all scoring Bill Gates bucks on their Internet start-ups). Theirs was an upper-middle-class struggle, and what other music goes better with this sort of existential angst than grunge? Black Sabbath played dark music that reflected the depressed nature of the factory town from which they emerged, so wouldn't it make sense for Soundgarden to play Sabbath riffs and discuss problems that were greater than themselves? It was living proof that no matter how educated or well-off you might be, everybody broods the same.

There is another level to the existential angst of the characters in *Singles*. It's based on a recurring image in the film that shows up and is referenced too many times to be accidental. It is an image that invokes a sense of personal longing and nostalgia for things that never happened (or only happened theoretically).

Steve has a postcard on the wall of his apartment of the *Kiss by the Hotel de Ville*, a famous photograph by Robert Doisneau. During his introduction, Steve describes the complications that arose with his last girlfriend and mentions that he wishes life were as simple as the photo on the postcard seemed to imply it could be. He sees the image as an idealized representation of how simple and straight-forward love can be. This is, of course, insane. As a thinking man's brooder, Steve should be thinking about how little he knows about the subjects in the photo and how little context there is. But he is swept up in those ideals, and that is quite telling.

It's natural for subsequent generations to feel nostalgia for the very recent past—it's why far too many people than logic would dictate never really get over high school. Psychologists have con-cluded that the growth of the current generation has been stunted because of information overload, so the emotional growth that was once expected at twenty-one is now delayed until twenty-five or twenty-six. While most of those people pine for the security or simplicity of their youth (even if what is defined as "youth" was only a handful of years ago), Steve in *Singles* does that concept one better and longs for a day, place, and time he has never even known. Clearly, he takes nostalgia very seriously. His stance speaks very acutely to the mentality of grunge listeners, both on an extremely personal level and on a sweeping, epic, generation-spanning level.

Steve deliberately sets himself up for failure, as even his most idealized relationship will likely never measure up to the bliss ex-pressed in his postcard. This is key—he is conciously setting up as-pirations to match or be better than the past, and he is knowingly failing. If there is one thing that Generation X took seriously, it was failure. Every generation wants to be better than the one that came before it—studies have shown that kids almost always as-sume that they will be better off than their parents—but Gen X ended up coming up short (at least from an economic perspec-tive). Of course, they had the deck stacked against them, as their parents were the so-called Baby Boom generation of postwar kids who were revolutionary in the sixties and seventies and then cashed a ton of checks in the eighties. It was an overwhelming standard to attempt to live up to, but because Gen X was overeducated and thus had taken plenty of psychology classes, they ended up setting themselves up for failure on their own terms. It's a brilliant strategy, really, and it permeated many aspects of everyday life and culture. What's the best way to not be disappointed at the end of the day? Keep your aspirations low and act like the underdog. Can't find a woman? Stare longingly at a postcard while acting hurt. Afraid your album won't be well received? Talk about how shitty your band is in interviews before anybody has the chance to hear you. Not making enough money? Start a Web-based company that doesn't really do anything and then shrug when the bubble bursts. It's a mentality that has taken the generation far, and they've basically never been held accountable. The bands from the era did the same kind of coasting—Kurt talked about how much he didn't like *Nevermind,* so whenever somebody actually brought up dissent (which was rare), he could say, "Of course— I told you that!" Steve puts up his own life against an ideal that is impossible to attain on several levels, protecting himself from profound hurt but disqualifying himself from the greatest heights, which sounds *exactly* like what it's like to be in Pearl Jam.

Of course, maintaining the middle of the road ended up sinking a great many alt-rock bands along the way. For a long time, anybody who had the audacity to declare themselves great was shunned and bands fell in line. After years of Bret Michaels crowing about the greatness of Poison, self-promotion was considered tacky and counterproductive to the ideals of what being "alternative" was all about. Bands, fans, radio jocks, and rock writers all fell into this trap in some way, and honestly, it made perfect sense. In an ideal world (again, the idealized reality rearing its ugly head, trying to be dragged into *actual* reality), self-promotion would be unnecessary. Being in an alt-rock band was sort of like being an overconfident communist—they all believed (or at least made everybody think they believed) that if they simply focused on their music and put out a great record, the cream would float to the top and all of the bad records would be eradicated by some sort of natural selection. Theoretically, this should work, and only "great" music would become platinum sellers and cultural phenomena.

Pop music is nothing if not wholly illogical, and there have been countless numbers of horrible things that became hits and wonderful things that got ignored. That's part of the fun of being a fan of indie rock: You can constantly argue that the stuff that isn't getting heard is far superior to the stuff that is, and not a whole lot of people can dispute you because *they* likely haven't heard that import-only Creeper Lagoon EP, either. Ideally, this makes you look both smarter and more attractive to the opposite sex. But for a while what was "underground" was actually in the mainstream, so those idealists thought that the tide was turning and that those ideals would permeate other areas of their lives. It's a sort of hell-freezes-over scenario—if Alice in Chains is being played *on the radio*, then why wouldn't everybody suddenly want to abandon their cars and ride a Super Train, as *Singles'* Steve believes? Though it seems naïve today, it made perfect sense in 1992. The fact that it *did* make sense and the sense that those ideals ultimately failed is why it seems so naïve now. The cast of *Singles* (and the people they represented on a larger cultural scale) can't say they didn't try, but they also can't say they made much progess. Such is the albatross of the generation—and it's an albatross that all the Mudhoney albums in the world couldn't carry.

OF COURSE, *Singles* is just a movie, and a fictional one at that. Cameron Crowe did not set out to make any sort of grand, sweeping commentary about the people of this particular generation; he really just wanted to make a movie about the difficulty of relationships that had his favorite bands in it. Still, because of the fact that the film took place in Seattle and featured some of the most popular bands at the time, *Singles* was absorbed (at least partially) as a sort of grunge-rock state of the union, and there was a great deal of backlash against it for those who didn't know the backstory. Though mostly irrational, the backlash did have a certain logic to it. Once you got past its grunged-up surface, *Singles* did not have anything that particularly grounded it in the alternative scene. Despite all that, *Singles* does have a legacy, as its sound track is considered to be one of the finest distillations of the burgeoning grunge/alternative scene on record. Amazingly, it not only managed to capture the bands that were popular at the time but also managed to have a sense of history and pay respect to some seminal influences, all in the span of thirteen tracks. In a few cases, a band's entire career, philosophy, and aesthetic were summed up in a single song. For instance, no song better represents Mudhoney than "Overblown," which manages to express their drunken pop sensibility, their signature sloppy riffs, and their shrug-and-sigh stance on the Seattle scene in less than three minutes.

The rest of the sound track delivers on all levels. "State of Love and Trust" is one of the five best songs in Pearl Jam's entire canon, "Birth Ritual" is Soundgarden's most successful fusion of Sabbath, Zeppelin, and the Beatles, and "Would?" featured a driving, anthemic riff and rightly became a huge single for Alice in Chains. But it's also important to acknowledge the contributions from Paul Westerberg, whose former band the Replacements was a seminal influence on the bands in the Seattle scene (the absent-from-this-discussion Kurt Cobain often cited the Replacements as one of his favorite bands). Westerberg's "Waiting for Somebody" acts as a sort of running theme throughout the movie, and it's got the same scratchy-guitars-plus-pop-sweetness chemistry that made so many other alternative bands such massive sellers in the early nineties. Despite *Singles'* poor showing at the box office, the platinum success of its sound-track album proved that while the audience had no interest in looking at fictionalized versions of themselves on the big screen, they still had no problem with those bands and their songs.

The critical and commercial backlash against *Singles* is a big reason that there simply are not very many films that belong to the grunge canon. The bands could sell albums by the truckload, but the audience did not want to see themselves or the bands they loved represented on the big screen. Even after grunge was dying, people stayed away, which is why 1996's documentary *Hype!* is one of the most important but unseen films of all time. Directed by documentarian Doug Pray, it features interviews and performances with just about every Pacific Northwest band that could have even marginally been called important circa 1992, from seminal heavy hitters such as Buzz Osborne, to pop stars such as Chris Cornell and also-rans such as the members of the Fastbacks and Seven Year Bitch, to total unknowns like Coffin Break. Though it's simply an oral history broken up by performance footage, it is an enlightening look into the mind-set of the musicians who made it, the ones who almost made it, and the locals who watched it all go down.

In *Hype!*'s various interview segments, the participants predominantly play down the attention that Seattle got at the height of grunge's popularity. Shot over a period of five years, *Hype!* captures all of the moods that permeated the emotional landscape. The sense of irony is heavy, suggesting that either everybody had a great sense of humor about the spotlight being thrown on the

Seattle sound or everybody was still trying to cope with that attention. It's a pretty healthy combination of the two. Many of the participants speak in a very shocked tone, as though they themselves are trying to process the success of their bands (or their friends' bands) in real time, and in many cases it's likely that's what was actually going on. The only people who really truly appear to have a clear perspective on the scene are Sub Pop founding fathers Bruce Pavitt and Jonathan Poneman.

The birth of Sub Pop is actually an interesting tale. Pavitt was a Chicago native who moved to Olympia to go to school and started a fanzine called *Subterranean Pop*. It gathered a fair amount of underground buzz, and the cassettes that Pavitt released with the 'zine were well received. Pavitt had a clear and incisive take on the American indie rock scene, which made him a perfect candidate to be the cool hunter running an influential label.

Pavitt was later introduced to Jonathan Poneman, who had read *Subterranean Pop* and was similarly interested in underground rock that was happening in Seattle and elsewhere. They formed the label in 1986, called it Sub Pop, and began putting out singles, establishing the wildly popular "Single of the Month Club." As they explain in *Hype!,* Poneman and Pavitt wanted the label to be a Motownesque enterprise, where the label name is as important (if not moreso) as the name of the band on the album. Incredibly, this line of thinking actually came to be, as a Sub Pop release was considered to be the mark of quality throughout the late eighties and early nineties. Sub Pop also provided an early home for just about every band that ended up mattering during the grunge era, including Soundgarden (their *Screaming Life* EP was one of the first releases for the young label), Nirvana, Screaming Trees, and Mudhoney. Though Pavitt and Poneman occasionally caught some flak from local Seattleites for seeming careerist, they do seem to possess a passion for the music. In fact, in *Hype!* they suggest what everybody was probably thinking: Despite the pose, a *lot* of those guys really wanted to be rock stars.

One thing that *Hype!* does express is the sense of kinship among the bands in Seattle during the grunge breakout. There is a very funny segment where an ancient-looking computer program is introduced that tracks where all the members of all the bands ended up playing and, as the overwhelming results make clear, just about everybody played with everybody else in town at one time or another. But in addition to the sense of mutual respect most of the musicians have for one another, there's also a strange sense of nostalgia that permeates *Hype!* Many of the bands talk about the good old days as though they happened aeons ago when in reality a lot of the events described occurred in the relatively recent past. When this is paired with the sense of too-early nostalgia in *Singles*, it starts to seem like a trend. It is for this reason that *Hype!* has actually improved with age, as the stories about the bygone era now make sense because the era is actually bygone now.

Hype! is a pure documentary, almost to a fault—it goes so far out of its way to avoid an editorial statement (outside of "Grunge is awesome," perhaps) that it seems a little wimpy at times. The performances are pretty amazing, and being able to observe the sort of fervor that was reserved for bands such as the Mono Men and Crackerbash is a treat. History has completely forgotten those groups (if they were ever remembered in the first place), but in Seattle they were absolutely rock stars, beloved by faithful clubgoers and other musicians alike. It illuminates the "why not us?" vibe of a lot of the bands that didn't break out as big as Pearl Jam or Soundgarden, as those bands didn't seem to have a greater following than anybody else. If anything, *Hype!* acts as a cautionary tale about the nature of fate in rock and roll and the danger that comes with a sudden blowup in a cultural scene. Taken that way, *Hype!*

(exclamation point included) might be the most appropriately named documentary of all time.

ESSENTIALLY, THE grunge era on film will be defined by the two aforementioned movies. Though *Hype!* engaged the bands and artists from the grunge era in the most direct way, it ended up saying the least about the culture and mentality of the people surrounding the music. Again, it's about the ideas. The albums will fade away, and the performances will seem more and more quaint (even now, it's hard to figure out exactly what the hell people were attracted to when it came to the bands in *Hype!*). But the sense of Sturm und Drang that permeated the minds of the young people represented in *Singles* resonates in a very profound and direct way. Though they are fictional, those characters don't have the same kind of complications that real people do; it's easier to digest and process the attitudes of those individuals when they are fictionalized. It's just another case where the truth is stranger than fiction, but the fiction is truer than the truth.

Attack of the Sasquatch Rock

THE PARTY LINE ABOUT THE SOUND OF GRUNGE INVOLVES THE bonding of punk and metal. On a macrolevel, this sort of dichotomy makes perfect sense, for most of the bands of the grunge era did indeed borrow the simplicity, attitude, and ragged first-take feel of punk and meld it with the muscle and noise of classic Sabbath metal. People point to the era's biggest band, Nirvana, as the anecdotal example, and at first glance that distinction fits like a glove, as the best songs from *Nevermind* are essentially just really slow punk songs (which is a distinction that fits bands like Mudhoney to a T).

However, certain bands skipped the "punk" side of grunge entirely and went right to gigantic, sludge-heavy riffs that formed dirgey metal tunes. It was the sound of arena rock made ungodly ugly. Alice in Chains did it with a little less notoriety (their success didn't come until they began to operate outside of their idiom; their most famous song is from an acoustic EP), but nobody did it better than the godfathers of a grunge subset known as "Sasquatch rock" (named for the legendary bigfoot that supposedly roamed the Pacific Northwest). If Sabbath was the heaviest of the heavy and Poison the glammiest of the glammy, then Soundgarden, those superheavy guys from Seattle, were the hairiest of the hairy. Their brand of arena-ready sludge rock was far more marketable than most of their contemporaries', thanks to Soundgarden's penchant for mammoth pop hooks and the wailing of Robert Plant–channeling front man Chris Cornell. They were even initially embraced by the same metal community that grunge destroyed. One of the first bands to establish themselves in the Seattle scene (two of their songs appeared on 1986's *Deep Six* compilation), they were also one of the last bands to implode under the spotlight. Ironically, Soundgarden gave birth to "alternative rock," a subgenre that eventually rejected them and sent them to an early grave in 1997 after a disastrous album and growing animosity between members. Soundgarden was a strange beast, but in the grunge era strange was the new mainstream and outcasts were the new cool kids, and for a handful of years in the early nineties Soundgarden was on top of the rock world and, despite selling platinum and attracting millions of fans, was still somewhat underappreciated and underrated.

OF ALL the bands that gained notoriety in the grunge scene, Soundgarden's rise to the top is the most traditionally archetypal. They are the only band to have formed in the pregrunge period, rise to stardom during the breakout heyday of the early nineties, and then manage to outlast just about anybody outside of Pearl Jam. During that time, Soundgarden did not particularly innovate or evolve a great deal, and since their points of reference were Black Sabbath, Led Zeppelin, and the Beatles, they always sounded like classic rock, even when they were new. There was nothing particularly fascinating about their approach, and their sound is not even very "indie" (especially considering the rock-star-god qualities of their front man), but Soundgarden became iconic in the grunge era anyway, and they did it *very* loudly.

The Soundgarden story actually began in 1981 in Illinois, where guitar player and beard aficionado Kim Thayil and bass player Hiro Yamamoto started playing music together in high school. The pair ended up at Evergreen State College in Olympia, Washingon, about an hour's drive southwest of Seattle, but quickly realized the city was where everything was happening (at least musically), so they moved there after a year, transferring to the University of Washington. Also along for the move was their friend Bruce Pavitt, who would later start up the fanzine *Subterranean Pop* and eventually cofound Sub Pop Records with Jonathan Poneman.

The members of Soundgarden first started crossing paths in bands in Seattle in the early 1980s. Yamamoto had joined a cover band called the Shemps that had put a "vocalist wanted" ad out in a local paper, and the guy the band eventually hired was a young drummer named Chris Cornell who wanted to try his hand at singing. The Shemps played mostly classic rock tunes (and by all accounts, they played the tunes relatively poorly). When Yama-moto eventually quit the band, bass-playing duties were taken up by his friend Kim Thayil. Cornell and Yamamoto stayed close, though—when the Shemps finally called it quits around 1984, the two moved in together.

Cornell and Yamamoto started jamming together and eventually brought along Thayil. In their earliest demos, Cornell channels Phil Collins by playing drums and singing at the same time. Eventually the band hired a drummer named Scott Sundquist to allow Cornell to concentrate solely on vocals. The three core members had all done time in classic rock–sounding outfits, but they were also into the noisy bands that were coming out of Seattle (they were fans of

Skin Yard, a band that featured eventual Soundgarden drummer Matt Cameron) and also dug the American Hardcore scene (they often expressed an affinity for Jello Biafra's Dead Kennedys).

The band decided to call themselves Soundgarden after a gigantic pipe sculpture that served as an outdoor art installation in Seattle. When the wind kicked up, it blew air through the pipes and made an incredible low-ended moaning sound; in the sonic sense, there was no more appropriate band name than that, as the band was an art project that also made ungodly, overwhelming sounds when the timing was right.

They began to gig around town, playing shows with the Melvins, Skin Yard, and a number of other early grunge forefathers. They formally recorded their first original material in 1985 for the *Deep Six* compilation, but Sundquist quit shortly thereafter to spend more time with his family. Matt Cameron left Skin Yard to join Cornell, Thayil, and Yamamoto in Soundgarden. Such was the sorta utopia of the Seattle scene—bands shared and swapped members constantly, with little animosity between them. It really was as though each musician was simply a member of a commune and that it didn't matter who they were playing with just as long as they were playing.

As the scene began to heat up in the wake of *Deep Six*, Soundgarden made history by becoming the first band to release an EP on the newly minted Sup Pop label, which was started by Thayil's old friend Bruce Pavitt. *Screaming Life* was released in 1987, and it's a remarkably accomplished piece of work. Produced by Jack Endino in only his second gig as a producer (he had previously turned the knobs for his own band Skin Yard on the *Deep Six* album), it's a little more straightforward than their later work, but it still manages to pack a pretty impressive punch. "Hunted Down," "Tears to Forget," and "Hand of God" all sound big and tough, and though Cornell hadn't quite found his wail yet (he sounds just slightly unsure of himself on *Screaming Life*), the mark of greatness was still apparent—in fact, the song "Nothing to Say" was once put on a local radio compilation titled *Bands That Will Make Money*.

The EP was well received, creating buzz not only for Soundgarden but also for Sub Pop. They released a second Sup Pop EP in 1988 called *Fopp*. In a sense, *Fopp* is something of a throwaway, as it contains only two original songs (fleshed out by a Green River cover and a dub version of the title track). But the strange funkiness of that dub tune revealed a side of Soundgarden that was simultaneously adventurous and somewhat goofy. It was an approach that defied conventions and created an atmosphere of unpredictability, which most of their mainstream contemporaries sorely lacked. Grunge bands did this remarkably well, but Soundgarden was probably the best at it. They were four hairy, strange-looking metal guys who played heavy riffs and sang about birth and death, but they also had a playful side. They weren't *funny*, per se, but as with many of the bands that shared their vision (and their performance spaces), a sense of humor was important. From the outside, it tended to give the impression that the bands weren't serious, which might have contributed to certain groups' inability to be taken seriously, like Mudhoney.

The thing that people tend to remember about grunge, though, is its heavy-handed moroseness. Pearl Jam has always been perceived as being "important," mostly because Eddie Vedder carried himself with such a profound sense of purpose. But Pearl Jam knew how to have fun, too, as evidenced by the white-boy funky *Ten*-era b-side, "Dirty Frank." Soundgarden ran into the same problems: They got famous for songs such as "Jesus Christ Pose" and "Black Hole Sun," but they also released a song called "Spoonman" as a single and recorded a track for their last album called "Ty Cobb," whose chorus was not about baseball but instead was Cornell intoning "Fuck you all!" with a sly grin.

So if there are all of these lighthearted indulgences on their résumé, why is Soundgarden remembered as the gloomiest of the gloomy?

Like most grunge bands, they were the victims of a perfect storm of assumptions. Though they toured the world, their music would always be defined by the city of Seattle, which from the outside is a pretty dreary place that has a very morose vibe. Sonically, they were also very dark, as even on the aforementioned "Spoonman" the guitars are distorted and sound sick in the "Touch Me I'm Sick" kind of way. But all sonics aside, Soundgarden and the rest of the grunge bands were seen as a reaction to the good-time hard rock of the 1980s. The perception about hair metal was that it was all about partying all the time, and for the most part that was true, even though bands like Twisted Sister and Judas Priest often ventured into darker territory. Since grunge was perceived as being the antidote to those kinds of rock poses, it clearly had to be the opposite of what that music represented. So even when grunge bands weren't sounding dour or morose or mournful or depressed during a particular song, it was assumed that they were only making time until they went back to being down. The accepted perception about grunge is that it killed off glam metal; by that logic, it would *have* to operate under the opposite pretense. If eighties bands were about partying, then nineties bands simply must have been about being bummed out. This is oversimplifying logic, but it's how scenes like this get reduced over time. In an age of information overload, things need to be consolidated and processed, so there's no room for nuance. By that token, all grunge bands were depressing all the time. Soundgarden? The most morose metalheads on the planet.

Though they could never have known it would eventually hurt (or at least limit) the perception of the bands at the time, a lot of those concepts came from the fans. Grunge was supposed to be a reaction to eighties metal in the sense that it was supposed to be *meaningful*, or at least smarter than your average Warrant song. There has long been a perception in the United States that being depressed made you smart, or at least made you seem smart. The sources are varied, but Woody Allen has a lot to do with it. Allen is a guy who is tremendously funny and dynamic and intelligent in his movies, but the characters were often in therapy or suffering some sort of existential crisis. In Allen's universe, being depressed meant that you thought more deeply about esoteric subjects like the expansion of the universe and this made you slightly more evolved than the person who didn't consider those things. It's a re-markably effective approach that a lot of young students take to heart. The best way to seem like a genius during your orientation week at college is to talk about your existential crisis.

Since the driving force behind grunge's first wave of fans was college students or twenty-somethings who considered themselves more advanced but couldn't get into Pavement, they naturally wanted their fandom to reflect better on them. Since people con-sider their favorite rock bands as an extension of their own person-alities (much in the same way people attach themselves to sports teams), the fans wanted to be perceived as smart or deep or mean-ingful for liking these bands. Since they were essentially big, loud rock groups, creating the perception that all these bands were de-pressed was the shortest distance to becoming profound. The bands themselves certainly contributed to this perception (as the music *does* sound pretty down), but the fans perpetuated it for the sake of their own identification. When Soundgarden or Pearl Jam or any-body else tried to goof around, the first people to naysay were the people who loved the band the most, as their goofing re-flected poorly on those same fans. It hurt the retroactive percep-tion of a lot of those groups, because many of them are now defined as being only one thing, but it probably got a bunch of twenty-something Seattleites laid in the process. Rock fans are nothing if not shortsighted.

BY 1988, Soundgarden had been receiving lots of attention from major labels, mostly based on the strength of the *Screaming Life* EP. Still, the band decided to put out their debut full-length on the independent SST Records. *Ultramega OK*, released in 1989, was really the first true "grunge" album to get noticed by the mainstream. *Ultramega OK* was even nominated for a Grammy (the first of the band's three career nominations). Despite the fact that it really represents Soundgarden finding their sea legs as the band they would·be known as, it is a very strange record for a full-length debut. The power is there, especially on "Flower" and "Beyond the Wheel," both of which are highlighted by Thayil's swampy riffing and Cameron's Armageddon-is-coming drums.

However, *Ultramega OK* contains two covers, a beefed-up version of Howlin' Wolf's "Smokestack Lightning" and a cover of John Lennon and Yoko Ono's "Two Minutes of Silence," which Soundgarden titled "One Minute of Silence" because they removed Yoko's part. The subversive Soundgarden sense of humor was present on *Ultramega OK* as well, in the form of "665" and "667," two tracks that reference the idea of metal bands being obsessed with the devil. The idea was that if 666 was the number of the beast, then the numbers on either side of it would have to be pretty powerful as well. The whole joke was tremendously high-concept, and the band even went as far as putting some backward messages on "665." However, when the song's messages are decoded, they aren't about Satan. They're about Santa.

Soundgarden's full-length release on an indie did not stop the major labels from continuing to make them offers, especially after the very low-budget video for "Flower" got a few spins on MTV.

Finally giving in, they signed with A&M Records in 1988, making them the first grunge band to get a major-label deal. While the majors had been interested in Seattle since the release of *Deep Six*, Soundgarden finally opened the floodgates for the feeding frenzy that would take place over the next several years. Soundgarden had been at it for years and was incredibly beloved in the Seattle community, so rather than cry, "Sellout," the other bands simply nodded and smiled.

The band headed straight back into the studio to record their major-label debut. The resulting album, *Louder than Love* (originally titled *Louder than Fuck*, then *Louder than Meat*), solidified the band as a driving force with a clearly defined sound. Because it was a major-label release, it also had major-label money behind it, so it was the best-sounding Soundgarden album yet, and the complicated nuances of Thayil's riffs and solos were finally highlighted properly. Though he often shunned the spotlight and subsequently was denied the credit he deserved, Thayil might have been the best guitarist (or most accomplished musician, period) of the grunge era. Look no further than the complicated time signature in "Get on the Snake" or the absolutely face-melting solo on "Gun" for proof. In a time period when chaos reigned supreme, Thayil added some style and grace to the proceedings.

Louder than Love is an excellent hard-rock record that contains some of the sharpest tunes in the entire Soundgarden catalog, especially the singles "Hands All Over" and "Loud Love." The album also contains another signature Soundgarden goof piece, this time in the form of "Big Dumb Sex," which was a painfully straightforward parody of all those eighties tits-and-ass songs (sample lyric: "I'm gonna fuck fuck fuck fuck you."), but played so straight that it's almost hard to tell if it's a joke or not. However, the lyric sheet is so over-the-top that it's almost impossible to process it as anything but a gag (as opposed to a similar song like Stone

Temple Pilots' "Sex Type Thing," which surfed the line between parody and reality a little too closely).

Shortly after the album's release and just before Soundgarden was about to embark on their first-ever big-time national tour, Hiro Yamamoto decided to leave the band to go back to school. Left hanging with a tour to get to, the band auditioned several bass players to replace Yamamoto. The band liked Ben Shepherd, who had played in a number of punk bands and was friends with drummer Matt Cameron. But Shepherd didn't know the songs well enough and wouldn't be able to learn them in time for the tour, so Soundgarden ended up hiring Jason Everman, whose most recent gig was as the second guitarist in Nirvana, but he was dismissed after the tour for *Bleach*. Everman's run in Soundgarden was extremely strange: Though he didn't play on *Louder than Love*, he is in most of the promotional photos from that era and appears in the videos from that record. The only thing he ever recorded with the band was a cover of "Come Together" (also featuring Jack Endino on backing vocals; it marked the last time Endino would produce Soundgarden) that appeared as the b-side to the "Hands All Over" single. Everman was fired after the national tour for *Louder than Love*. It's clear that the guy was a total disaster, as he always managed to be unceremoniously canned from seminal acts (he later dropped music altogether and joined the army; it's assumed he's had better luck there).

Despite Everman, the tour for *Louder than Love* was a big success and *Louder than Love* managed to crack the Billboard charts. When Soundgarden returned home to Seattle, they hired Shepherd to come play bass and work on their next album for A&M, which would be titled *Badmotorfinger* and be released in 1991.

Before the release of that album, however, the band was sidetracked by the overdose death of Mother Love Bone front man Andrew Wood. Wood was a good friend to both Cornell and

Thayil and had even been Cornell's roommate at one time. The news of Wood's death hit the Seattle community hard, and hit Soundgarden especially hard. They had lost their founding bass player and had now lost a dear friend and musical ally. In response, Cornell rounded up his friend Stone Gossard, also of Mother Love Bone and soon of Pearl Jam, and collaborated on a handful of songs that were recorded with Pearl Jammers Jeff Ament, Mike McCready, and Eddie Vedder, along with Cameron and Thayil from Soundgarden. The group called itself Temple of the Dog, and the resulting self-titled album became the first album of a grunge supergroup, even though neither band had gotten much exposure as of yet. But when A&M formally released it in 1991, it became a hit and ended up spawning the radio and MTV hit "Hunger Strike." In fact, "Hunger Strike" ended up being the first time mainstream audiences really got to see and hear Chris Cornell and his epic set of pipes.

In retrospect, 1991 might have been the biggest year in music history. While it saw the breakout of grunge in Nirvana and Pearl Jam, it also featured the return (and subsequent collapse) of Guns N' Roses and saw the breakouts of Garth Brooks and Amy Grant and the death of Freddie Mercury. For Soundgarden, it meant the release of their best album yet. Though it was overshadowed a bit by the breakout successes of fellow Seattleites Nirvana and Pearl Jam, *Badmotorfinger* still scored several radio hits in "Rusty Cage," "Outshined," and "Jesus Christ Pose." It got built up over time, but it eventually ended in the Billboard Top 50 by 1992, right around the time Nirvana and Pearl Jam were both peaking. Though Soundgarden had both of those bands beaten in terms of longevity and depth of catalog, they were still not considered to be "elite" yet (that wouldn't come until the release of their next album). It seemed for a while that while Soundgarden was building a fan base and getting more and more success, the overwhelming wave of pro-Seattle sentiment didn't appear to be rubbing off on them. Considering they had been slowly building themselves up since 1984, it's likely that they would have had the same level of success in '91 as they would have if Nirvana never appeared. The sudden Seattle blowup should have made them kings, but for a brief moment it looked like they were going to be relegated to bridesmaid status.

Nobody could ever accuse Soundgarden of being lazy or complacent, as their touring schedule for *Badmotorfinger* was long and grueling. The band spent almost a year straight on the road, opening dozens of shows for Guns N' Roses and Skid Row in late '91 and early '92 before spending the summer of 1992 on the main stage of the second annual Lollapalooza tour (along with Pearl Jam, Red Hot Chili Peppers, and Ministry; there were also a few sets by Temple of the Dog, marking some of the few times those collaborators played live). Soundgarden's sweat and toil paid off, though, as playing for so many different types of rock fans and staying on the road made *Badmotorfinger* into a platinum album. MTV was also sitting up and taking notice, spinning the videos for "Jesus Christ Pose" and "Outshined" during the summer of 1992.

The standout detail about *Badmotorfinger* is that it really represents the pinnacle of Chris Cornell as a singer and a front man. The album fully celebrates and exploits his otherworldly wail, but it also highlights the soulful croon that he had developed and that the band would later ride to pop crossover status. Songs such as "Outshined" were given a new dimension that balanced out the brutal, jagged noise of the song with Cornell's rich vocal stylings. In fact, the definitive Chris Cornell vocal track might be on "Birth Ritual," the song the band provided for the sound track to Cameron Crowe's *Singles*, a movie in which the band also appeared. "Birth Ritual" is everything that's great about Soundgarden: the tough riffs, the heavy rhythm section, and Cornell's rock-god vocals that equally call to mind the seering tenor of Robert Plant and the booming baritone of Jim Morrison. It's a dichotomy that is unfortunately not always associated with Soundgarden. Of all the grunge bands, they are remembered perhaps as the most monochromatic. Though they released a number of singles that showed a great deal of variation, they are recalled as the big, dark metal band of the grunge era.

It's easy to make that mistake, though, as Soundgarden's next album, which catapulted them to pop stardom, was also their darkest. Sounding more like Black Sabbath than Sabbath themselves, *Superunknown* was Soundgarden's finest hour and also its biggest hit. Released in 1994, *Superunknown* went straight to the top of the Billboard charts and went platinum five times over. Its singles included the freewheeling, wacky "Spoonman," the pitch-black ballad "Fell on Black Days," and the anthemic "The Day I Tried to Live." But the one song that defined *Superunknown* and subsequently will represent Soundgarden until the end of time is a hot slab of Beatleish psychedelic metal called "Black Hole Sun."

"Black Hole Sun," which would win a Grammy for "Best Hard Rock Performance," was a massive watershed moment for grunge, sadly occurring at the end of its reign of supremacy in the post-Cobain era. The song was a massive molten slab of melodic rock, a midperiod Zeppelin riff wrapped in a wave of druggy psychedelia. The lyrics seem to be about Armageddon (or some sort of cataclysmic event that seems pretty biblical), and the words match up perfectly with the music underneath, as the tension and discomfort in the verses give way to the bombast and destruction in the chorus. Curiously, "Black Hole Sun" is one of the few Soundgarden songs that follow the traditional quiet verse/loud chorus dynamic that grunge made famous—the band always seemed to go from being loud to being extremely loud.

A big part of the success of "Black Hole Sun" (and of *Superunknown* in general) was due to the video, which was in the most popular clip on MTV in the summer of 1994 and later won an MTV Video Music Award for "Best Hard Rock Video." In a series of Lynchian images, a cavalcade of demented-looking people with hideous smiles make their way around a highly stylized neighborhood as the sky turns black and the gates of hell threaten to open. There is a woman cutting up a still-flopping fish in a kitchen, a group of religious types encouraging people to repent, and, in the most surreal twist, a little girl who turns a plastic doll on a spit over a grill and later lets melted ice cream drip from her mouth in a tremendously disturbing image at the song's climax. It's a video that remains both cool-looking and affecting and still shows up on MTV "Best Of" countdowns.

In fact, "Black Hole Sun" was just one of the many excellent videos produced by grunge bands during the early nineties. From 1991 to 1995, music videos were at their peak of artistic prowess, and grunge bands led the way. The videos produced in that era were done by the first wave of directors who would later cross over into feature films. Guys such as David Fincher, Mark Romanek, and Anton Corbijn really came into their own during the grunge era, crafting interesting, compelling videos that featured images that sometimes lasted much longer than the bands associated with them.

The quality of the videos came from several different driving forces, the first of which was money. People often forget that the art of music videos was still relatively nascent in the early nineties, as MTV had not even celebrated its ten-year anniversary by the time the decade started. But in that time MTV had proven that they had the ability to break bands (and in the time before the Internet they were just about the *only* entity that could make or break a record). The early nineties also saw the beginnings of MTV branching out into other nonmusic forms of programming (most notably *The Real World*, which debuted in the summer of 1992), so for a video to get airtime it had to grab the attention of the viewer (and the MTV programmers) that much quicker. So by the early nineties, labels were willing to throw a lot more money at the production of a video in hopes of getting it on MTV, breaking new bands and sustaining older ones. More money meant more options, which allowed directors to dream bigger and make their clips feature-length-quality narratives. In many cases, music videos had finally evolved into high-quality short films.

But it wasn't just the directors and big checks from labels that made grunge-era videos great—the bands also had a lot to do with it. A lot of bands from the alternative era came from artier backgrounds and had a strong visual sense (Kurt Cobain, for example, fancied himself a painter). They wanted the visual representations of their songs to be as strong and striking as the songs themselves, so they drove an aesthetic that encouraged everybody to think more outside the box.

Videos also became artier based on necessity. Since a lot of bands shunned the spotlight, videos had to come up with alternatives to simply showing the band playing the song, which led to a greater sense of narrative in videos and more of a focus on striking visuals. Though they are present in the clips, nobody really recalls the images of the bands in the videos for "Black Hole Sun" or "Heart-Shaped Box" or "Jeremy." Those videos all seem to be drawing focus *away* from the band so that the focus can be on the song and the story in the clip.

For a while, it seemed as though the music video existed as more than just an instrument of hype for a band or a record—it was an art form unto itself. Like everything else in the grunge era, it didn't last long, as the rise of bling-heavy hip-hop and sugary pop in the latter half of the decade returned videos to their hype-machine quality. But also like everything else in the grunge era, it was amazing while it lasted.

"BLACK HOLE SUN" and *Superunknown* were the climax of Soundgarden's career; unfortunately, things tumbled in the years after. They released their final studio album, *Down on the Upside*, in 1996. Though it received a great deal of critical acclaim and earned Soundgarden a lot of respect for trying new sounds and experimenting with things outside their idiom, it was a commercial disappointment, and its creation led to tensions within the band about a new direction. They once again set out on a grueling touring schedule, playing a number of European festivals and making another run on the Lollapalooza tour. But the tensions bubbled over at the final show of the tour in 1997. Frustrated with a reported equipment failure, Ben Shepherd stormed off the stage and left Chris Cornell to perform the encore by himself. Two months later, Soundgarden announced their breakup, keeping up with the grunge tradition of passive endings. They were the last of the *Deep Six* bands to fall, and they made a hell of a run of it.

Matt Cameron ended up joining Pearl Jam on drums, and Kim Thayil and Ben Shepherd both have appeared in various projects. Cornell released an acoustic-tinged solo album in 1999 that sounded like an unplugged Led Zeppelin album. He later shocked the universe by joining up with three of the four members of Rage Against the Machine to create Audioslave, a postmodern aggro-rock band with the funky guts of Rage Against the Machine and the epic vocals of Cornell.

There was little about Soundgarden that wasn't archetypal. Their sound adhered closely to the prototypical sound of grunge that took a handful of metal riffs, messed them up, and added a little punk attitude (though Soundgarden was, as stated earlier, easily the least punk of any of the grunge bands, no matter how many Dead Kennedys shows they attended). Their rise to fame was a slow burn, and they broke out about the same time as the rest of the Seattle hit makers (though their truly big success came a bit later). Even their breakup was grunge-by-numbers: Although there was news of tension within the band, they essentially just shrugged and went their separate ways. They were really the workingman's band–they did a lot of things really well but probably never anything spectacularly but also never really bottomed out. They never had drug problems or courted a great deal of controversy. They never had spectacular personalities. They simply lived the grunge ideal: They showed up, they rocked, they thanked their fans, and they went home. Soundgarden dared to live the dream, and because of that they were the *most* grunge of anybody–sonically, socially, and philosophically. They'll be remembered as a big, hairy, loud metal band, but they were actually the grungiest of the grunge.

CHAPTER 9

—

OUTSIDERS AND WANNABES

Hitting Poses, Cashing Checks

ANYBODY WHO EVER PLAYED ORGANIZED SPORTS SHOULD BE FA-
miliar with a cliché that typically goes like this: "The team is only
as strong as its weakest link." This sort of catchphrase is always
thrown around by coaches during team meetings in order to give
the kid at the end of the bench a sense of self-importance and to
make him feel more involved in the production of the squad (especially if a team is successful). In reality, the whole concept is
crap, because sports teams don't rely on their worst players to do
much of *anything.* During Michael Jordan's legendary run of six
championships with the Chicago Bulls in the nineties, Phil Jack-
son never drew up clutch plays for journeyman sharpshooter Jud
Buechler, mostly because *Michael Jordan was on the team.* In fact, the
"weakest link" concept is unfair to great performers, as it suggests
that the less talented will bring them down to their level, rather
than be elevated by their greatness.

Unfortunately for grunge bands, the cliché is truer than most
would like to admit. Certainly the first bands that everyone remembers are the legends: Nirvana, Pearl Jam, and Soundgarden. The
greatness of those acts has been well established and will likely

compound with time. But defining the era based on the work of those bands is useful only to a point. Their sounds did establish and define what it meant to be a rock band during that particular era, but at the same time they have been put so high on a pedestal that it is almost impossible to process them as bands, as they are greater than simple rock groups. They are icons that represent not only music but also fashion, philosophy, and a greater social aesthetic. *Nevermind* ceased being simply "a great album" years ago when it became a lightning rod for an entirely new and specific set of attitudes that mean more than simply twelve guitar-based songs.

So without the cornerstones to judge, the burden of history falls on the me-toos, the also-rans, the Johnny-come-latelies, and the wannabes. It's unfair to go through this exercise, mostly because these albums are generally inferior by design (if they were better, the bands would have transcended their status and joined Nirvana and Pearl Jam as icons), and history will likely correct this over time—after all, who remembers the lesser painters of the Renaissance? The only guys still mentioned are the legends—nobody ever brings up the fifteenth-century Italian equivalents of Candlebox, whomever they may be.

But as terrible (or at least as less inspired or less transcendent) as many of these albums are, they are still important. They might not have a great deal of sway over the greater annals of rock history, but they did contribute a great deal to the story arc of grunge. It's also interesting to note that not only have a handful of these bands survived to the current day, but several have remained *successful*, as illogical as that may seem. History rewards greatness, but as *Amadeus* has taught us, sometimes the mediocrities are the ones who shape things in greater ways than anybody is willing to admit. This is their story.

—

ASK ANYBODY who has a knowledge of grunge to describe the archetypal early-nineties front man, and a few recurring themes tend to arise. They will likely describe a white guy in his twenties who had a rough childhood. He will be moody and sensitive and prone to fits of self-involvement, and he'll sometimes be bitingly sarcastic and achingly sad, and all he really wants to do is rock. People who describe this particular guy will assume they are describing Kurt Cobain or Eddie Vedder, but really they are describing Billy Corgan. Though Corgan's band was from Chicago, sounded almost nothing like the bands coming out of Seattle, had no real punk-rock roots, and actively sought out to become huge rock stars, the Smashing Pumpkins' front man was one of the greatest and most influential icons of the alt-rock era.

Smashing Pumpkins began in Chicago as a collaboration between Corgan and his guitar-playing friend James Iha. The Pumpkins were influenced heavily by the Cure, and their early songs channeled the sad-eyed goth rock of bands such as Bauhaus and New Order. They were joined by bass player D'Arcy Wretzky, and the group began gigging around the Chicago area playing shows with a drum machine, which was later replaced by jazz drummer Jimmy Chamberlain, whose bombastic style would shape what Smashing Pumpkins would sonically evolve into.

Buzz grew after getting an early rub from Jane's Addiction, and the band was signed to Virgin Records in 1991. Butch Vig, who had produced Sonic Youth and who would later go on to produce *Nevermind*, sat behind the boards for the band's debut album, *Gish*. An accomplished but confounding debut, *Gish* is a collection of fuzz-filled, dreamy, driving rock songs that didn't sound like anything that was being played on the radio yet still seemed like it was arena-ready (mostly due to Chamberlain's absolutely massive drum sounds). In the pre-Cobain indie era when *Gish* was released, it was deemed a massive success. Smashing Pumpkins toured America and saw their popularity rise exponentially. Their video for "Siva" was getting spins on MTV's *120 Minutes* (later they would become staples on the early-nineties MTV cornerstone *Alternative Nation*), and there was talk of Smashing Pumpkins being the band that could really break through and redefine the rock landscape.

Gish was released in May of 1991, but when Nirvana broke in September of that year, the spotlight shifted to Cobain and the rest of his Seattle brethren, leaving Corgan and the Pumpkins temporarily on the outside looking in. Corgan felt slighted; he felt even more slighted that Nirvana had taken Butch Vig, the same producer who helmed *Gish*, and catapulted him into the stratosphere. Suddenly Vig was an alt-rock tastemaker, and with *Nevermind* storming the charts, *Gish* never got the sort of attention it deserved.

After ending their tour on a bit of a whimper, Corgan and the Pumpkins set about making their follow-up, the album that would truly tattoo their name on the mainstream consciousness. The record would solidify Corgan as a genuine genius, blow the doors open for what sounds were acceptable on an alternative-rock album, spawn countless imitators, and become one of the most successful albums of the grunge era. Corgan called the album *Siamese Dream*.

Siamese Dream is a stunning collection of thirteen songs that took Vig's crisp, clean, arena-ready production on *Nevermind* and elevated it to the nth degree. It took the basic sounds of *Gish* and filtered them through a pristine seventies rock sensibility. It's a record full of tracks that are meant to be heard in stadiums. "Rocket," "Cherub Rock," and "Today" all became modern rock radio staples, and it is not hard to see why: Each of those songs has the quiet verse/loud chorus dynamic that all grunge exploited, plus a killer hook and Corgan's whiny, wistful vocals that still commanded a great deal of attention despite their obvious short-comings.

But the Pumpkins weren't just crafting perfect arena anthems—they were also experimenting. Though its pop sheen has become its dominant trait as time went by, *Siamese Dream* actually contains several experiments and risks that were pretty amazing and outside-the-box circa 1993. Most notably, the heavy orchestration of "Disarm" was indeed disarming, as its strings and bells swelled and crashed over a simple acoustic loop while Corgan intoned the ominous refrain: "The killer in me is the killer in you." In fact, "Disarm" represents the pinnacle of a type of song that was not necessarily birthed during the grunge era but certainly found its home: the Creep Rocker.

Creep Rockers didn't always have similar sonic characteristics, but they did always share thematic elements—namely, the lyrics always discussed what a jerk/freak/creep the singer was, and always in the first person. Sometimes they were ballads, like Stone Temple Pilots' "Creep," but sometimes they were loud, distorted rockers, like Silverchair's "Freak." Before they became humanized versions of music-making robots, Radiohead broke out during the grunge era with their Creep Rocker, which was also called "Creep."

These songs all seemed to draw inspiration from the first generation of creeps: Morrissey, Robert Smith of the Cure, and Trent Reznor, all of whom had goth leanings and pretty bad self-esteem problems. It was a match made in heaven, as most of these musicians either were prone to self-flagellation (like Corgan) or at least realized that self-flagellation was an excellent marketing tool (like Scott Weiland; see elsewhere in this chapter for more on the horrors of Stone Temple Pilots). Creep Rockers were definitively grunge (most of Hole's *Live Through This* is made up of them), and they were even passed on to the next generation, as Creed's breakthrough hit was about Scott Stapp condemning himself to a self-made cell in "My Own Prison." In an era of profound self-loathing, the Creep Rocker found its home among the unwashed slackers of the nineties. Since nobody was allowed to have fun anyway, everybody figured they might as well figure out what their problems were, and wouldn't you know it? They often found those problems inside.

RELEASED IN the summer of 1993, *Siamese Dream* was the third alternative album to truly transcend traditional classifications. While Nirvana and Pearl Jam claimed various classic and underground rock influences, *Siamese Dream* had no interest in sounding "underground." Rather than channeling Pixies or the Melvins (as Kurt Cobain often claimed), Billy Corgan seemed to be channeling Boston and Journey, bands whose historical significances are not entirely dismissed but certainly in question. Corgan took a lot of heat at the time, and historically the heat appears to have only gotten greater, as *Siamese Dream* is often dismissed as a lesser album than it actually is. Plenty of people branded Corgan a sellout, but he absolutely made the album he set out to make, and considering the climate of rock circa 1993, it's possible that the most "alternative" thing a band could do was make a naked bid to be on the radio.

Siamese Dream was not without other controversies. Stories surfaced that Corgan had played every note of the album himself, or he had rerecorded D'Arcy Wretzky's bass lines, or he had exiled the rest of the band from the studio. The stories still conflict, but Corgan does insist that every band member was playing on the album every day in the studio. The idea that Corgan does not play well with others certainly stuck, though, as his relationships with

Wretzky and James Iha deteriorated, and Corgan's post-Pumpkins band Zwan also apparently broke up because of personality issues between Billy and other band members. But Corgan was the same moody perfectionist as Kurt Cobain—the only difference is that Corgan's band was given time to fall apart.

Also like Cobain, Corgan never really did the same thing twice. The follow-up to *Siamese Dream* was a tremendously ambitious two-disc concept album called *Mellon Collie and the Infinite Sadness*. There were some classic Pumpkins rockers present, such as "Zero" and "Bullet with Butterfly Wings," but it was predominantly made up of epic art songs like the treacly "Tonight, Tonight" and synth-heavy workouts like "1979." When Corgan fired Jimmy Chamberlain after his drug habit got out of control (and led to the death of Smashing Pumpkins' touring keyboardist Jonathan Melvoin), he decided he didn't need a drummer and made a Depeche Mode album, which he called *Adore*. Reaction to it was mixed at best. He welcomed back Chamberlain for the Pumpkins' swan song, *MACHINA/The Machines of God*, which got back to their early roots but put more of a Kissesque metal tinge on the songs. *MACHINA* was largely ignored and represented Smashing Pumpkins' ultimate demise.

Corgan's solo work and his pseudoreunion of the Pumpkins may sully his personal legend status, but the legacy of Smashing Pumpkins cannot be denied. They released one of the most important albums of the era, and though it flew in the face of the indie-first conventions at the time, it still made its mark and was the sort of mainstream rock album it was still okay for smart, sensitive people to like, and that's because the band had a smart, sensitive front man in Corgan. Their commercial success was nothing to sneeze at, either, as Smashing Pumpkins managed to pull off stunts that no band today would even think of attempting, never mind managing to succeed. In 1996, in the wake of the massive success of *Mellon Collie and the Infinite Sadness*, Corgan put together a box set of all five singles from that album ("Bullet with Butterfly Wings," "1979," "Zero," "Tonight, Tonight," and "Thirty-three"), gave each of them a couple of b-sides, and sold it as a rarities set. It was a five-disc batch of leftovers from a single album, and it nearly went gold. Who else can claim that level of absurdity?

IN 1992, the familiar strains of a deliberate, distorted guitar riff could be heard coming across radio waves and cascading all over MTV. The song was clean and intense and was anchored by the heavy baritone of a soulful front man. It sounded like Pearl Jam's second album would be just as good as—if not better than—their first one, especially considering the newfound sexual energy they seemed to be exuding.

Vs. did end up being great, but the song that everybody heard wasn't Pearl Jam—it was "Plush," the debut single from a group from San Diego called Stone Temple Pilots.

Stone Temple Pilots was formed when singer Scott Weiland met bass player Robert DeLeo at a Black Flag concert. The two began making music together as Mighty Joe Young. Drummer Eric Kretz and guitarist Dean DeLeo, Robert's brother, joined soon after to make up the only lineup STP ever had (how very un-Seattle of them!). The band settled on the name Stone Temple Pilots after discussing favorite decals from their youth, when Weiland came up with a play on the old STP motor oil logo (though the first idea was Stereo Temple Pirates). The band quickly gained buzz around Los Angeles and San Diego and signed to Atlantic Records in 1991.

Up until Bush showed up to ape *Nevermind*, Stone Temple Pilots were the definitive wannabes. Journalists and media critics were absolutely ruthless with them and derided them for their old-style rock-and-roll swagger and their single that sounded exactly like

Pearl Jam. Whether or not STP's intentions were good is irrelevant, but their debut album, *Core*, was victimized a bit by the single-selection process. While the whole record does sound a little too close to a Southern California band trying to sound like a Seattle band, "Plush" is by far the worst offense. STP would have likely met with the same sort of judgment no matter what their first single was, but they were certainly dealt a bum hand when the record label chose "Plush."

It hardly mattered, of course. The will of the people was not to be denied, and people went absolutely apeshit for STP. *Core* sold over 8 million copies in the United States alone on the strength of *five* singles, and "Plush" won a Grammy for "Best Hard Rock Performance." If rock writers were ever looking for evidence of their absolute irrelevance, they had to look no further than Stone Temple Pilots, who were absolutely raked over the coals and managed to conquer the world regardless.

MTV went especially nutty for the boys in STP. With Pearl Jam shunning videos and Nirvana becoming more difficult, Stone Temple Pilots provided a straightforward, visually interesting rock solution that lit up the airwaves. MTV gave the band their own *MTV Unplugged* special and aired countless news pieces about how they had formed and what they were up to. The videos for "Plush," "Sex Type Thing," and "Creep" were all in heavy rotation throughout 1992 and 1993, and they featured front man Weiland looking not very grungelike at all. He was a theatrical, pose-heavy lead singer—a true rock-and-roll front man in the tradition of Jim Morrison. Weiland was moody and esoteric, yes, but he also knew how to command a crowd and knew the power of his genitalia.

Core is a pretty derivative album that doesn't just rip off Pearl Jam but also borrows from sources as far-reaching as the Psychedelic Furs and Blue Oyster Cult. The singles are the whole story—there's the slow grind of "Plush," the definitive Creep Rocker

"Creep," and the possibly misogynistic, definitely confusing "Sex Type Thing." Weiland came under a lot of fire for the lyrics of "Sex Type Thing." He claimed that it was meant to be a story song and that he was inhabiting a character. That's a lazy way for rockers to pawn off controversial lyrics on fictional people, but Weiland meant it, going as far as sometimes wearing a dress onstage when the band performed the song. Retrospectively, the lyrics to "Sex Type Thing" are so deliberate and over-the-top that you have to *hope* that Weiland didn't actually mean them, lest he need serious professional help.

After collecting their Grammy and their *Rolling Stone* reader's poll award, both for "Best New Band," they returned in 1994 with *Purple*, supposedly written and recorded in under a month. Stone Temple Pilots had gone through a magical transformation that saw them truly come into their own as a band. The songs on *Purple* have little to no connection to the grunge scene, as STP's new sound was equal flashy glam and edgy psychedelic rock. There were still a couple of Pearl Jammy moments—most notably the riff on "Meat Plow" and the changes on "Pretty Penny"—but *Purple* also delivered "Interstate Love Song," an Eagles-esque blast of juiced-up California rock that has zero relationship to anything Pearl Jam or Soundgarden ever produced. It's an airy, smooth rock song with an unbelievably catchy hook and Weiland's affected rasp in top form. Though the Seattle rockers ruled the roost, "Interstate Love Song" tops everything else from the entire alternative universe not called "Smells Like Teen Spirit."

Just because Stone Temple Pilots were emancipating themselves from their grunge influences didn't meant they didn't still indulge in some bad grunge ideas. They were constantly on the verge of being completely derailed by the drug problems of their singer, Scott Weiland. Like his colleagues from the Pacific Northwest, Weiland's poison of choice was heroin, and his troubles began in

1995 when he was arrested and charged with posession (his first of many arrests while in STP). Fearing their singer's legal troubles would ruin the band, Stone Temple Pilots separated for a while before Weiland rejoined the band in late 1995 to record its third album.

Tiny Music . . . Songs from the Vatican Gift Shop from 1996 is as weird as it's title suggests. Though it was produced by Brendan O'Brien (who had also produced STP's first two albums), it sounded like an entirely different band at work. The heaviness in Dean DeLeo's guitar was almost gone, replaced by a sort of aggro jangle that chugged along on the uptempo rockers and eased up to create atmosphere on the slow stuff. The first single, "Big Bang Baby," is one of the glammiest tunes STP ever produced, with a robotic riff over hand-clappy drums and Weiland's high-fashion vocals. The singer's drug problems were peaking during the recording of this album, and it's readily apparent in the songs, as this is the druggiest-sounding record the band ever produced (even more so than their next album, *No. 4*, which seemed to be actively attempting to be druggy).

Though STP was evolving, they still were wholly dismissed by critics but generally endorsed by fans. Rock writers were apparently completely unforgiving of the "Plush" transgression, as every permutation of Stone Temple Pilots was panned and sent packing as unimaginative dreck.

Weiland's drug problems continued and the band parted once again, allowing Weiland to record the superweird solo album *12 Bar Blues* and the rest of the band to collaborate with Ten Inch Men singer Dave Coutts as Talk Show. The one Talk Show album is one of the most laughable side projects in history, with uninspired cookie-cutter tunes that seemed to send the STP concept backward several steps in the evolutionary process. Coutts was especially embarrassing, as his attempts to avoid sounding like

Weiland resulted in him sounding like he was trying to sound like Weiland. The whole album is a mess, and the brothers DeLeo are probably relieved that it has gone out of print.

Stone Temple Pilots reunited in 1999, but things were never the same. Their fourth album, *No. 4*, sputtered commercially because (1) Weiland was in rehab during the time the band should have been touring and (2) it's not very good. The band went for Beatle-esque simplicity on their fifth and final album, *Shangri-La Dee Da*, in 2001, but it was the sound of a band trying to fulfill their contractual obligations. They disbanded shortly after, and Weiland joined Slash and a bunch of other Guns N' Roses castoffs in Velvet Revolver, one of the worst hard-rock bands of all time, especially considering the pedigrees of the members. The brothers DeLeo worked on other people's albums before forming Army of Anyone with Filter front man Richard Patrick, while Kretz runs a recording studio in Los Angeles.

Stone Temple Pilots probably never deserved a fair shake, but people seemed especially eager to go out of their way to make sure STP never got one. While Weiland rarely stayed out of trouble long enough to tour properly, there was rarely a band that was better at giving the fans what they wanted than Stone Temple Pilots. In that respect, they are sort of like grunge's version of Cinderella or Ratt–nobody every took them seriously, but they made a handful of more-than-competent records and always gave the audience what they were looking for. Stone Temple Pilots may have been wannabes, but they were tremendously conciliatory wannabes.

WHILE Stone Temple Pilots could be forgiven for their transgressions, there is no forgiving Gavin Rossdale's band Bush. Debuting in 1994 with their album *Sixteen Stone* and the tremendously Nirvanaesque single "Everything Zen," the Bush band members were ridden mercilessly as the posiest of all the posers. They were art school students from England—what did they know about the Seattle rock they were so accurately aping?

But once again, the populace spoke with their wallets, and Bush was a massive hit, selling millions of albums and becoming modern rock staples in the post-Cobain era. The funny thing was that everybody seemed to process Bush as a Nirvana clone—nobody *ever* acknowledged the band without bringing it up. In fact, it was the first thing their fans would readily admit. Bush became an extremely meta-experience, where everybody was in on the joke but played along with the game anyway.

Sometimes it seemed like even Bush was in on the joke. Though Rossdale constantly deflected the criticism with his chiseled cheekbones, Bush occasionally came across as a very elaborate art experiment. For example, the single "Little Things" was probably the most naked aping of "Smells Like Teen Spirit" ever written, but Gavin liked to deflect that observation by claiming that the song was a lift . . . of the Pixies' "Gouge Away" (which, consequently, was the same riff that Kurt likened "Smells Like Teen Spirit" to).

Or a better example: In 1996, Bush went into the studio to record their second album, titled *Razorblade Suitcase*, with Steve Albini, the same gentleman who had produced Nirvana's *In Utero*. With all of the accusations of Nirvana-aping that Bush received, you would think that they would want to create a bit of aesthetic distance between them and Kurt Cobain for their second album, but you'd be horribly wrong. There's no possible way that Rossdale did not consider at some point in the process that the news of Albini's production would cause a massive backlash and even more name-calling and dismissing, so Rossdale was either (1) unbelievably self-confident in his wishes to work with whomever he wanted to work with, the rest of the world be damned, (2) calculated in his attempts to make Bush into less of a band and more of an art experiment (where the experiment was apparently "do what Kurt did"), or (3) unforgivably stupid and naïve. It's hard to tell what was the case, but Albini took the job, and his production style makes *Razorblade Suitcase* sound a lot like *In Utero*. Rossdale may have been able to replicate Cobain's vocal style but could never mimic his sense of pathos. But if the whole thing was meant to be a joke, Albini seems exactly like the type of maladjusted guy to help a too-clever British dude carry it out.

Razorblade Suitcase became a hit, spawning a couple of singles and a handful of weird videos, but grunge was already fading and making way for a more aggro brand of rock. But in 1997 the whole world assumed that electronic music would be the next big thing and that kids the world over would trade in their guitars for samplers. This is how desperate people were to crown rock stars and icons in the post-Cobain world—they were going gaga over *DJs*. The Chemical Brothers were being played on MTV on a specially designed show called *Amp*, and the Prodigy graced the cover of *Spin Magazine*, who crowned them the next big thing. It was an incredibly overblown time that saw very little good music, and none of the so-called stars of the electronica movement did much in the way of actually delivering a new electronic rock hybrid.

That didn't stop Bush, however. They released an album of remixes titled *Deconstructed* in the fall of 1997 to a mostly apathetic response, and they followed that album up with a somewhat aggro, somewhat electronic *The Science of Things* in 1999, which met with a similar response. *The Science of Things* contains elements of electronic music but hints at a nü metal influence as well, bridging the gap between the two predominant next big rock things at the time. Bush's career wrapped up in 2001 with *Garden State*, an album that was somewhat well received but fell on mostly deaf ears (though it got a bit of attention when the band changed the title of the first single from "Speed Kills" to "The People That We Love" after the September 11 terrorist attacks). Bush was unbelievably guilty of bandwagoneering, but was it all intentional? It's hard to decipher, but judging from the subsequent work Rossdale has done with his new band, Institute, it seems as though all of his moves with Bush were legitimate.

It is doubtful that any band will ever be as derivative of another band as Bush was of Nirvana. That fact alone makes Bush's existence remarkable. While the music may have been unoriginal, it's hard to deny the nastiness of some of Bush's hooks, and even Courtney Love admits that "Machinehead" was one of the better rock songs of the nineties (even though it is the least grungy-sounding track on *Sixteen Stone*, sounding much more like a wussed-up Judas Priest cover than anything Nirvana ever did). Gavin Rossdale shouldered the burden of a lot of things he shouldn't have had to, like the death rattle of the music we call grunge. He might not have killed it off for good, but he certainly didn't help the cause. But in a time when grunge was dying anyway, why not grab the last scraps left before the ship sank? The nineties were supposed to represent ideals greater than that, and therein lay the big problem with Bush: They were opportunistic in a time when that was considered crass and horrible. If only Gavin had been born fifteen years earlier and joined Def Leppard—then he'd be remembered as a rock god.

THERE WERE plenty of other bands besides Smashing Pumpkins, Stone Temple Pilots, and Bush that scored big-time success while getting a shine from the grunge movement, even though none of those bands had a whole lot of association with the Seattle rock heavies. The breakthrough of those bands really marks the transition from the concept of grunge to the broader genre of alternative rock.

But there were countless other groups that popped their heads above water and got a bit of one- (or two-) hit-wonder love from the grunge masses and then dipped back down below, likely never to be heard of again. Candlebox was probably the most notorious of these groups. Their debut album was prototypical grunge: quiet verses, loud choruses, and an anthemic sense of self-loathing. The guys even wore flannel and looked like auto mechanics. Candlebox's two singles, "Far Behind" and "You," are the type of songs that will pop up on nineties retrospective compilations until the end of time, because they are immediately recognizable when they begin and absolutely forgettable once they end. Candlebox came under a bit of fire because a story came out that suggested that Candlebox had been an L.A. band that had moved to Seattle specifically to cash in on the grunge scene. That story proved to be untrue, as Candlebox played the same Seattle clubs in the late eighties and early nineties as Soundgarden and the members of Pearl Jam. But the amazing thing is that once that perception was out there, people were unwilling to believe anything else. It is for that reason that unless their front man finds a universal cure for cancer during a reunion show, Candlebox will go down in history as "that band who moved to Seattle so they could be grunge." Anybody looking for evidence that grunge fans were an unforgiving sort need look no further than the Candlebox parable.

Another band that was nakedly derivative of grunge (and Nirvana in particular) was Silverchair. Made up of three teenagers from Australia, Silverchair might as well have been a Kurt Cobain tribute act, as they had it all: the song structures, the Kurt vocalization—even their name was a reference to a Nirvana lyric. Their debut, *Frogstomp*, is one of the worst albums of the nineties. It makes Bush and Stone Temple Pilots look like the Beatles and the Stones. The songs are cookie-cutter and boring, and it's not even produced well, despite knob twiddling by Aerosmith producer Kevin Shirley. Critics rightfully hated it.

Against all odds, Silverchair managed to improve on their subsequent albums, where they morphed into a tougher, heavier alternative band, even gathering some critical praise for their trippy, sorta-metal 1999 album, *Neon Ballroom*. Silverchair is a perfect example of how bands seemed to leap over each other in an attempt to become more like the breakout bands from Seattle. It wasn't just a matter of making the same sounds so they could sell the same records and make the same money. Nirvana, Pearl Jam, and others carried themselves with a sense of integrity that remained intact despite the commercial windfalls. It was as though every rock band on the radio had also figured out how to be U2, staying classy and cashing checks with minimal questions or interference. For young rock bands, that sort of success is the holy grail. It's having your cake and eating it, too. That carrot must have seemed far too great an opportunity to pass up, especially to an eighteen-year-old with a distortion pedal.

The irony is that by aping somebody else these bands had no shot at ever attaining any kind of integrity, mostly because grunge audiences were too smart (and too vindictive). Silverchair managed to dust themselves off and grow into the band they would have become anyway, while others had mixed results.

Rock radio was littered with wannabes, which are a necessary evil in any cultural movement. After all, somebody had to flesh out the playlists when the Nirvana tunes fell out of rotation. Bands like Sponge, Better than Ezra, and Collective Soul had to exist, even if they didn't really offer anything new. Ironically, the benign groups might have been able to extend their careers because they were so benign, but it's the spectacularly derivative bands that gained a place in history. People will always have a hard time remembering whether it was Dishwalla or Our Lady Peace who sang "Counting Blue Cars," but the tales of Gavin Rossdale's artistic indiscretions will be told as long as there is rock music. After all, if you can't be the best, why not fail spectacularly?

CHAPTER 10

–

APRIL 1994

The Beginning of the End of the Beginning of the End

PEOPLE LOVE TO REINVENT HISTORY; MUSICIANS, ROCK JOURNAL-
ists, and music fans seem to have a particular affinity for it. Nowadays, fans talk about the breakup of the Pixies as a huge historical
moment that rearranged people's perspectives on music, personal
relationships, and culture as a whole. But considering their record
sales and relative popularity, reality dictates there were barely
enough people who even knew who the Pixies were to care about
their breakup, let alone enough to spread that sort of news around
to other people. The folks who bought *Surfer Rosa* were probably
bummed out, provided that they realized the breakup had even
occurred (this was before the Internet was in everybody's homes
at all times). People remember the date Frank Black sent his legendary fax because they heard about it later; on that particular
day, 99.9 percent of the Pixies' fans went about their routines as
though their favorite band were still together.

This same sort of revisionist history occurs when people talk
about the single biggest moment in the history of grunge: the
death of Kurt Cobain.

The day that Kurt died (or rather, the day the public found out he was dead—coroners said he had already expired two days prior to his body being found) is, in truth, one of the most unifying moments in rock history. His death represented something that couldn't be defined, but people immediately knew that it was going to be a major generational moment. This is not all that unusual—when Elvis died, fans who had long sworn him off were willing to put aside the fact that he had become a disgusting, bloated parody of himself and wanted to submit him for sainthood. People forgot about the fat drug addict Elvis in the same way they forgot about the ornery drug addict version of Cobain— the day he died, people remembered the closing shot of the video for "Smells Like Teen Spirit." It's a cliché that dying young is the best way to preserve your legacy, but it's also a pretty easy way to *sanitize* your legacy (unless you're Layne Staley, and then dying young only confirms how unbelievably fucked up you really were).

Kurt enjoyed a similar kind of instant revisionism. In the months leading up to his death, the general public had begun to sour on the man who had been delivered to them as the savior of rock and roll just three years prior. The diehards stuck with him and Nirvana still had no trouble selling albums, concert tickets, or T-shirts, but the tide of popular opinion was turning. It probably didn't help that *In Utero*, the follow-up to their breakout album, was one of the most alienating and difficult commercial rock records ever recorded.

Almost as soon as *Nevermind* was released, Kurt began to turn on it, and when "Smells Like Teen Spirit" blew up, his resentment of his own work kicked into overdrive. Unhappy with the shiny pop sheen placed on the final tracks at the hand of mixer Andy Wallace, Cobain often complained that the sound of his commercial breakthrough was "too slick." For the follow-up he wanted something that sounded raw and live and difficult, and there hasn't been anybody in the music world who fit that description better than Steve Albini.

Albini, best known as the founder of such "difficult" (read: noisy and adored by rock critics) bands as Big Black, Rapeman, and Shellac, also became known as the king of minimalist producers. Cobain was obsessed with Nirvana sounding raw and ragged, and Albini's methods suited him quite nicely. The resulting album, *In Utero*, became one of the strangest pop records ever made: brutally honest, directly anticommercial, and somehow still irresistible.

In Utero opens with a single downbeat that acts as a mission statement for the remainder of the disc. The hum of an amplifier and the sharp sound of drummer Dave Grohl counting off with his sticks give way to an aggressively strummed chord that drifts out of tune. The main guitar line then kicks in amid a wash of stray notes and feedback. It's the sound of suffering, of an old man gasping for air, wheezing his last breath. Only then do Cobain's vocals kick in, announcing the second mission statement in about twenty seconds: "Teenage angst has paid of well," but Cobain was sick and tired of it. If there was ever a guy who wanted to drive a stake through the heart of the entire grunge movement, which seemed to be swelling with juvenile suffering, it was king Kurt himself.

Cobain spends most of the rest of *In Utero* trying to distance himself not only from his peers but also from his own back catalog. While the themes on *In Utero* are not exactly fundamentally "adult" (after all, on the chorus to that opening track, "Serve the Servants," Cobain declares, "I miss the comfort in being sad," which was likely ironic but does suggest an attachment to pubescent *malheur*), they could certainly be considered "elevated." "Heart-Shaped Box," the first single and video, is about Kurt's complex relationship with Courtney Love—a relationship far evolved past the basics of older songs such as "About a Girl." "Frances Farmer Will Have Her Revenge on Seattle" also goes the elevated route, referencing a local Seattle legend of a woman who went mad. "Pennyroyal Tea" is, at least on the surface, about abortions. While some of Cobain's penchant for the surreal and knack for word association still existed, these were lyrics that were focused, and they were delivered with very little postproduction, per Albini's style—only after the label's insistence did famed R.E.M. producer Scott Litt come in and sweeten the vocals on the single.

Cobain matched these intensely personal, elevated themes with music that was nothing short of punishing. For an album that has never been considered metal, it's brutally hard. The guitars regularly sound de-tuned, the bass gurgles and farts, and the drums are far too loud thanks to Albini's microphone systems. But despite its harshness, it is also remarkably well paced. The pauses for prettiness (the verses of "Heart-Shaped Box," all of the cello-fueled "Dumb," and most of the closer, "All Apologies") serve as an ideal respite from the noise. But like the calm in between heaving when you have food poisoning, it's just as deceptive and quickly gives way to more torrents of Armageddon. The combination of Cobain's raw, stripped-down, and direct songs and Albini's spare, leave-in-all-the-mistakes production style churned out an album that was capable of literally turning stomachs.

But it wasn't just that Nirvana had released a difficult album. Cobain's behavior had become more and more erratic in the months prior to his death. There had already been one apparent suicide attempt while on tour in Rome, where Kurt took a bunch of painkillers and chased them with a bottle of champagne. The remainder of that tour had to be canceled, and the Cobain camp claimed that his near death was entirely accidental. When he returned to Seattle, he entered a rehab facility after an intervention led by Love. Two days later, he escaped and once again returned to Seattle, where he went AWOL until he was found dead two weeks later.

Like most suicide notes, Cobain attempts to explain a lot without giving away too many clues about his motives. He opens it by calling himself "an experienced simpleton" and claims the note "should be pretty easy to understand." Cobain's main argument appears to be that he simply didn't enjoy writing and performing anymore. Not only did he feel joyless, but he felt totally disconnected from his audience and from most of the people around him (the word "empathy" appears several times in the note, and it appears to be a sensation Cobain believes he is not capable of feeling). The note is also pretty self-deprecating. About halfway through, he stops and says: "Jesus, man! Why don't you just enjoy it?"

The tone of the note is pretty spot-on with Cobain's character. Though he is saddled with being the Grand Wizard of the New Age of Irony simply because he was the most recognizable figurehead of that generation, Kurt was actually alarmingly genuine–the only real irony is that nobody took him seriously. He consistently reminded people that he had no interest in being a star, yet because Kurt was supposed to be ironic *all the time*, people assumed he really wanted to be huge but was altruistically declaring that he didn't. When the legend is broken down, it's amazing how disconnected he and his fans really were, and though there were legions of people out there who hung on his every word, no one seemed to really understand where he was coming from.

One person who *did* understand him pretty completely was Courtney Love. It's hard to imagine considering her actions over the past fifteen years, but there was a time when Courtney Love wasn't famous. In fact, Kurt's death was the first time most people had considered Courtney on a macrolevel. There were probably some people who had liked Hole's debut album, *Pretty on the Inside*, but since that record was mostly unlistenable and commercially non-existent, the first time most of the nation heard Courtney's voice was when she read the suicide note over a loudspeaker during the daylong vigil for Cobain. Depending on who you ask, that vigil was either a heartfelt tribute attended by an artistic collective of the world's greatest music fans or a pack of punk kids looking to glom onto a zeitgeist they had nothing to do with creating, bound simply by counterculture, loud music, and the idea that Kurt's suicide was somehow cool. In the thick of it all stood Courtney. Clearly, she had a very dubious entrance.

Psychologists say the first stage in the process of mourning is denial (typically followed by anger, bargaining, and finally acceptance). When celebrities die (and *especially* when rock stars die), this process tends to happen in reverse. Acceptance always seems to come first, and it always seems to be the thing that people carry. When Tupac Shakur was shot to death in Las Vegas in September of 1996, his death was met with outrage and sadness. After the mourning period was over, however, the conspiracies started to roll in: Tupac was murdered by associates of his cross-country rival, Biggie Smalls; the hit was ordered by Death Row Records CEO and all-around bad guy Suge Knight; the CIA killed Tupac because he had somehow figured out who shot JFK. Following that, the popular opinion was that Tupac had staged his own death and that he was still alive, even after photos of his autopsy leaked on the Internet. Of course, Elvis Presley is the be-all and end-all of this sot of treatment: As soon as the King was buried, people started spotting him at truck stops in rural Tennessee. Sometimes hero worship is so strong, it can raise the dead.

No one appears to be claiming that Kurt Cobain still roams the earth, but conspiracy theories surrounding his death started to roll in shortly after the mourning period had ended. Mostly people were in denial that Kurt would take his own life. They believed he was dead, but they also believed that he had been murdered. People also started pinning motives on Courtney Love, accusing her of driving Kurt to do himself in.

In truth, Courtney was dealt a pretty miserable hand. When Hole's sophomore album, *Live Through This*, came out only days after Cobain's death, Love was accused of being an opportunist, capitalizing on Kurt's demise in order to sell records. Of course, the release date had been set months prior. Courtney also came under fire when several pieces of paper containing handwriting samples were reportedly found in her backpack the week of the suicide. The samples appear to be of somebody attempting to ape Kurt's handwriting, suggesting that Love herself might have penned Cobain's suicide note.

No matter how much time is given for healing purposes, there will always be a handful of people who will still hold it against Yoko Ono for breaking up the Beatles. Just like Yoko, Courtney will always have some blame pinned on her, in this case for the death of alternative rock's most iconic figure. No formal accusations have ever been levied against Love, and Cobain's death certificate cites "suicide" as the cause of death.

IT'S UNFORTUNATE that it carries the sort of baggage it does, but it's still amazing that *Live Through This* is regarded as a classic. Though it's rarely allowed to stand on its own (people tend to think of it as the immediate fallout of Kurt's death and not as an album by a band called Hole), Courtney's sophomore effort is by far the best and most complete musical statement she has ever made (and considering her recent output and lifestyle, it looks like it will stay that way). *Live Through This* seems to channel every countercultural musical movement of the early nineties and distills it into radio-ready (but still wholly abrasive) rock-and-roll moonshine.

Despite the success of *Live Through This* (which spawned the radio and MTV hits "Doll Parts" and "Violet") and the generally positive reaction it received in the press (*Spin Magazine* named it the best album of the year), Courtney still had a pretty terrible 1994. There was Kurt's death and the backlash and frenzy that went along with it, but she suffered another loss that was just as important to her. On June 16, Hole bassist Kristen Pfaff was found dead in her bathtub. Official reports showed that the twenty-seven-year-old musician had accidentally overdosed on heroin. Pfaff and Love had already gone through a falling-out following the completion of the album, and Pfaff had moved to Minneapolis for a while to play with an old band of hers called Janitor Joe. She had returned to Seattle to collect the last of her belongings, and she reportedly was to have left that afternoon.

Pfaff was replaced by a Canadian bass player named Melissa Auf Der Maur. Auf Der Maur had played in a Montreal-based band called Tinker, which had opened for the Smashing Pumpkins in 1993. Pumpkins front man Billy Corgan had stayed in touch with her and suggested that she could fill Pfaff's position. Auf Der Maur initially balked at the job but later decided it would be a good opportunity and joined Hole two weeks before the Reading Festival. Later, before striking out on her own as a solo artist, Auf Der Maur seemed to make a habit of filling in for departed female bass players, as she filled in for embattled Smashing Pumpkins bassist D'Arcy Wretzky in 1999.

PERHAPS IT'S the remoteness, or perhaps it's just a knack for grandiose storytelling, but many of the events that make up Seattle's social history tend to be exaggerated. For example, in 1999 the city played host to a summit held by the World Trade Organization. For many, the WTO represents evil on a number of different fronts: corrupt businessmen, the exploitation of workers, shady backroom government deals, worldwide poverty, and the oppression of women. Naturally, such a summit was subject to protests by various local groups, and the protests became the definitive news cycle story of the week. But while images on TV and descriptions on Web sites made it sound as though the proletariat was finally rising up to slay their monarchs, in actuality the "riots" were relatively contained and actually pretty small by protest standards. All in all, they were just another example of media embellishment– making a mountain of trouble out of a couple of malcontents at a Starbucks. In the age of hyperaccelerated media, this sort of thing happens all the time. But it's worth noting that the grunge era existed right on the precipice of that on-demand universe, which makes any indulgent stories of that nature from that era subject to social history and word of mouth, not coverage on Fox News and entries on Wikipedia.

A similar sort of historical anomaly crops up when people look back at the vigil held for Kurt Cobain on April 9, two days after he was found dead at his home in Seattle, the victim of a well-placed shotgun blast through the back of his head. The images broadcast by MTV News that day suggested a massive throng of people from all walks of life coming together to mourn their fallen icon, as Cobain was arguably the most famous resident Seattle had boasted in decades. The vigil was punctuated by an appearance by the widowed Courtney Love, who read Cobain's suicide note aloud over a public-address system. The images remain emotional and powerful, if only because attendees still seem to be working through shock– they have not yet advanced past the denial stage of mourning.

Of course, time has treated that event slightly differently. As it turns out, the Cobain vigil, while powerful in its own right, was not a unification of Seattle or a coming together of disparate groups via the power of grunge and legacy. As it turns out, the majority of the attendees that day were kids from the suburbs dropped off by their moms in minivans, who also brought their skateboards to mourn. What is remembered as a powerful coming together might have been more of a middle school field trip.

Now, this niggling fact may come across as an ageist judgment on the ability of teenagers to process both pop music and death, but the fact that the kids showed up is almost beside the point. The significance lies in the shifting of the story over time, which speaks of a more emblematic problem with the grunge era: the dramatic shifts in historical significance.

As was stated earlier, grunge rose and fell just before the big information technology boom of the nineties, but it was deeply affected by the already-ingrained acceleration of culture that made the Internet such a necessary breakout piece of technology in the first place. The early nineties were the dawn of the era wherein any piece of culture—especially pop music—is considered, processed, labeled, and reevaluated almost immediately. Downloading, clearinghouse review sites, and personal blogs have made this possible, and today a band will be packaged and placed in a cultural context before anybody has ever heard the music. In 2004, everybody knew exactly what the Arcade Fire represented before anybody had heard a single song—indeed, the music became almost beside the point. What mattered became not what it was but what it meant and represented. The criterion for loving a band used to be "Does it rock?" In the twenty-first century, it's "Does it mean more than music?"

This is one of the reasons the grunge era is fascinating not so much as a movement unto itself but also as a transition period between the metal era and the modern day. When really broken down into components, grunge makes no sense: It was loud metal-inspired riffs, played with more focus on the visceral than the intellectual, and yet it was glommed onto not only by the mainstream but by the pop culture intelligentsia as well. Grunge was declared meaningful in the way that metal never could be—it was allowed to exist outside of itself. Metal existed as songs and bands; sometimes it seemed like grunge existed only as concepts. Grunge bands represented abuse, or the dangers of success, or the struggles of women, and it was all done on purpose. A band like Poison certainly ended up representing the dangers of success, but that was entirely accidental and retroactive—it's hard to believe that was Bret Michaels's original goal.

The irony of it is that the paradigmn didn't shift entirely—it's not just as though suddenly all great records had to be grunge records (whereas in 1997 it seemed as though all great albums had to have at least a peripheral relationship to electronica in order to be considered outstanding). Seminal indie acts such as Pavement and Liz Phair all broke ground during the grunge era and in their most notorious incarnations never sounded like they belonged anywhere, yet it wasn't unusual for somebody in 1992 to be discussing Pavement's *Slanted and Enchanted* and Alice in Chains' *Dirt* in the same conversation. It's not that they had crossover fans (something that seems predicated on little more than wildly divergent personal tastes and sheer luck), but it's that those albums were given the same amount of cultural weight. *Slanted and Enchanted* couldn't do anything but exist outside itself and got on college radio anyway, while *Dirt* was designed to be played in arenas but really got people thinking about the horrors of heroin addiction and the ravages of post-traumatic stress disorder. It was an amazing time to be a rock fan—in the present tense, at least.

But here's where the problem arises: Over a decade later, *Slanted and Enchanted* is written about as though it's a precious classic from another universe, while *Dirt* does not appear to have retained any of its social cachet (nobody appears to be itching to give it a deluxe reissue, as Matador did with *Slanted and Enchanted* in 2002). Is this because Alice in Chains is seen not as a seminal band but merely as a successful also-ran? It's possible, but that likely feeds into the larger problem: Grunge has not aged well, at least in the minds of those who bother to keep track of such things.

As a practical example, grunge very closely resembles the punk movement of the 1970s, at least on a macrolevel: It was antisocial music practiced and embraced by young people as a symbol of rejection of bloated corporate rock. Each genre had its core members (Nirvana and Pearl Jam were more or less stand-ins for the Sex Pistols and the Ramones), with a ton of peripheral acts that also achieved success (Beck, for example, should be considered the modern-day version of Talking Heads, because both are groups that shared stages with musical movements, grunge and punk, respectively, and aligned with those bands aesthetically, even if they had next to no relationship musically). Plus, both grunge and punk had somewhat vague, formless endings, mostly starting with the downfall of their two flagship bands (Nirvana and Sex Pistols).

Ask any critic about seventies punk, and he or she will talk about the importance of the bands, the impact they had every time they played CBGB, and the influence they've had over music in general for the past twenty-odd years. Grunge does not elicit that same sort of response. In fact, even for a casual fan, saying you're into grunge is like saying you enjoy Gregorian chants—sure it was big once, but what has it done for you lately?

THOUGH THE musical genre he was most associated with now seems stodgy and outdated, Kurt Cobain's death still stands as one of the most iconic and defining moments of a generation, simultaneously killing grunge off and making it immortal. There wasn't another great grunge album made after Kurt's death, but the ones that came before shimmered a little bit more once he was gone, especially his own albums: It's doubtful that *Nevermind* would still be considered the touchstone that it is had the brains behind it not been shot out of Cobain's skull. *Nevermind* certainly still rocks, but outside of "Smells Like Teen Spirit," it's not terribly meaningful (and "Teen Spirit" is only meaningful because of the fervor that surrounded it, not because lyrics are rife with meaning), though it does remain *important* for those same contextual reasons. Kurt's musical output remains impressive, and he certainly knew how to *rock*, but the weight given to his back is almost certainly overblown. By the end, Kurt himself had written off *Nevermind* as "too slick," and it's likely he would have grown unhappy with how *In Utero* was softened up in the mixing process. It's likely that Cobain would have evolved into another Jandek or Captain Beefheart, spending most of his time on a commune painting and only emerging once in a blue moon to make a strange folk album or play the odd concert. He would have still been labeled a genius, but he would have always been qualified as "Salingeresque."

But the fact remains that Kurt did make a dramatic exit. So what is his legacy outside of himself? More important, keeping in step with the overanalysis that was a major part of the grunge era, what did Cobain's death *mean*?

For many, Kurt's death represented the ultimate failure of his ideals. Especially when viewed in the context of the note he left behind, Cobain's suicide marked the impossibility of living out the ideals that he had. Kurt tried hard to remain "alternative," even in the face of critical and commercial acclaim, but in the end it proved to be impossible. Of course, this is an extremely underevolved position to take, as there were many other circumstances that contributed to his ultimate end. Cobain didn't kill himself simply because his fame became overwhelming, but on the surface that appeared to be his entire motive for offing himself, and that is where his legacy gets complicated. It ended up painting Cobain as a tragic figure–which, by all accounts, he *was*–but it also set the precedent that even our greatest torch-carrying heroes were doomed to fail.

Oftentimes when rock fans debate the end of grunge, much is made of the fact that nobody really stepped up to take the symbolic helm after Cobain passed on. Kurt was the clear figurehead for the grunge movement, and without him nobody stepped up to stand in the spotlight as the new cornerstone of the movement. Eddie Vedder, who was always unwilling to embrace the spotlight, had already begun his antifame campaign with Pearl Jam. By mid-1994, they had already stopped making videos and were touring less and less because of their budding conflict with Ticketmaster. For a time, it looked like Soundgarden was going to take the reins, as their greatest and most successful album, *Superunknown,* was released merely a month before Kurt died. But despite the size and volume of the band and the fact that they sold 20 million records and had a massive crossover hit with "Black Hole Sun," Chris Cornell never seemed like a leader, mostly because he was so soft-spoken and had become hyperaware of the sort of tolls success could take on a musician, especially on his friend Andrew Wood. Soundgarden certainly was huge, but they were not going to lead rock to the promised land, nor were they going to carry Cobain's mantle.

The only other character who seemed like a logical heir to the alternative throne was Billy Corgan. Though his band Smashing Pumpkins was not from Seattle and their sound was big and loud but shared little sonic quality with their Seattle counterparts, they were still given the spotlight as part of the alternative pantheon, based mostly on the critical and commercial success of their 1993 album, *Siamese Dream.*

In fact, of all the guys who were brought up as possibilities for a new alternative figurehead, Corgan seemed like the most logical, if only because he had so much in common with Cobain. Both Kurt and Billy came from broken homes and experienced difficulties growing up in underprivileged suburban America. Later they both started their musical careers on indies and then graduated to the big leagues. They even both had relationships with Courtney Love.

But Billy was also known as a difficult, misunderstood iconclast. He was often called a control freak, and there were rumors that Corgan had played all of the tracks on *Siamese Dream* himself because he was not happy with the performances by bandmates James Iha and D'Arcy Wretzky (both Corgan and Pumpkins drummer Jimmy Chamberlain deny this). Corgan generally got along with the press but often came across in interviews as crass and coldhearted—though these comments were rarely meant to be malicious. Like Cobain, Corgan simply could not turn his honesty off, which was sometimes interpreted as boorishness or pigheadedness.

Ultimately, Corgan was too fragile for Cobain-size levels of fame. Corgan even made a Cobainesque move by releasing a very difficult follow-up album to his band's breakout. *Mellon Collie and the Infinite Sadness*, released in the fall of 1995, was a sprawling two-disc album that incorporated the classic Pumpkins sound of "Today" and "Rocket" but also brought in orchestral rock, complicated prog, brutal metal, electronic sounds, new wave, and copiously quiet, delicate ballads. The album ultimately sold millions and spawned several hit singles (including "1979" and "Tonight, Tonight," both of which were very esoteric and nontraditional rock radio songs), but it was not the kind of record that led a revolution, if only because it contained a song called "Porcelina of the Vast Oceans" (though that isn't all that much stranger than "Francis Farmer Will Have Her Revenge on Seattle").

Corgan ended up being a hell of a rock star—even now he still garners attention, despite the fact that the critical reaction to his post-Pumpkins projects has been mixed at best. But he's no Cobain, and therein lies the problem not only with the alternative movement but with popular music on the whole: People were actively searching for "the next Nirvana." Even today, journalists, record executives, musicians, and fans still use that phrase, which when extrapolated basically means that they are searching for a band that will break out from the underground and command the attention of everyone at once. However, since everyone now recognizes that such a phenomenon is *possible*, those same people are actively on the lookout. But if people are seeking out bands that can break into the mainstream, the process of that breakout cannot happen as organically as it did with Nirvana. Cobain and company were special because their rise was so unexpected and unlikely. When rises to fame become constructed, the performers become no better than any other pop songstress or R & B crooner shoved down the throats of consumers by record labels and publicists. The very awareness of Nirvana's history has tainted the process they went through, making it a one-time-only deal.

For forensic proof, take a simple observation of the new rise of indie rock that began to occur at the turn of the millennium. Spearheaded by bands such as the Strokes, the White Stripes, and Interpol, the new indie movement (sometimes referred to as the "small band" movement or the "new garage" revolution) was an attempt to capture the spirit and energy of the alternative scene that broke out a decade prior. Though those bands saw some success, they did not see the sort of mainstream exposure that the alternative bands had. Most everybody saw right through the ruse—these new bands were marketed as having bubbled up from under, but the ploy was too constructed, too corporate. It started a precedent that now sees bands getting "underground" hype (typically through blogs, Webzines, or other Internet outlets), but by the time their album is released, burnout has already occurred. To record executives, hype is hype, but music fans have grown smarter since the Nirvana days. They recognize that the hype surrounding the grunge groups (at least the first wave, anyway) was organic, and they also recognize when they are being bullshitted. Unfortunately, sensitivity to bullshit tends to lead to cynicism, which makes *everything* seem like bullshit.

All this can be traced back to the grunge era. Through circumstances entirely out of their control, one of the many legacies of alternative rock bands is the slow death of honesty and earnestness. One of the bluntest, most genuine movements in music history ended up giving way to its spiritual opposite. Kurt died, grunge died, and honest integrity died with it. Even though he was a true rock star by the time he passed on, Kurt represented the embodiment of what it meant to stick to your guns and play by your own rules. Though grunge still had a few years of life left in it, Cobain's death was certainly the event that kick-started the Rube Goldbergian process that saw alternative rock collapse in on itself and give way to the splintered indie rock and metal scenes that took over the rock landscape. Rock history is littered with self-destructive fallen idols—Elvis, Hendrix, Elliott Smith, and the rest—but no single musician's death has ever had more far-reaching ramifications on music and culture than Cobain's. Even if he had gone into hiding and become a hermit, it's still safe to say that rock and roll misses the guy badly.

—

EPILOGUE: THE NEVER AND THE NOW

ONE OF THE MOST PROBLEMATIC ISSUES WITH THE GRUNGE ERA IS defining when it ended. Just as grunge ended metal, some other genre should have come along and laid grunge to rest with the crushing blow of a watershed record. Unfortunately, nothing of the sort happened. In fact, grunge wasn't even overtaken by one definitive genre—the focus of pop music fans became sugary sweet Swedish concoction care of boy bands and starlets, while guitar music was being usurped by bands such as Korn and Limp Bizkit in a genre that became known as nü metal. But there was no single album or group that came along to declare dominance over the rest of the radio landscape; rather, these bands simply showed up and began feasting on scraps, blocking out whatever demographics they could get their hands on.

Though it may be forgotten to history (especially by those responsible for it), there was supposed to be a new definitive youth movement genre that ignited the underground and invigorated music fans. Much like grunge, it even had a silly and reductive name: electronica. As people grew tired of big guitar rock in the midnineties, it was widely assumed that DJs would be the new

rock stars and rave kids would be trendsetters for the next generation of music fans. Massive sums of money were poured into artist
development; guys such as Roni Size, huge among dance enthusi-
asts but unknown to anybody who wasn't addicted to Ecstasy, suddenly found themselves with major-label deals. The media bought
into it as well, as rock magazines were suddenly featuring multi-
page profiles of guys such as Goldie and Tricky, who openly
admitted to having no musical talent at all. Many of them were anti-
musicians, which made sense—after half a decade of guys in bands
taking everything as seriously as a heart attack and being hyperaware of their credibility, the idea of music whose goal was nothing more than to inspire you to move seemed like the most
refreshing concept in pop music history.

Unfortunately, electronica was not all that it was cracked up to
be. Though a handful of breakout personalities made their way
into the mainstream (most notoriously the Chemical Brothers, Fat-
boy Slim, and the Prodigy), most of the highly touted albums of
the genre were commercial flops. The music-buying public was
not willing to watch videos of amorphous blobs on MTV2 (though
there were some definitive clips made, like Aphex Twin's "Win-
dowlicker" and Spike Jonze's various projects for Daft Punk) and
was also unwilling to go to a concert that featured a group of guys
with their heads down, focused on computers. People had grown
tired of grunge's sweaty visceralness, but the extreme swing toward the antiseptic turned out to be a miscalculation.

SO WHEN did grunge really end? There are multiple arguments. In
theory, the whole genre should have imploded on itself when Kurt
comitted suicide in 1994. There was no longer a leader (at least fig-
uratively) or a trendsetter to keep everybody on their toes and
ahead of the curve. Plus, looking at it retroactively, all of the genre's

best and most defining albums had been released by January 1, 1995. In fact, perhaps the only truly defining albums of the grunge era released after Kurt Cobain ended his own life are Pearl Jam's *Vitalogy* and Hole's *Live Through This* (which, of course, came out the Tuesday after he died, though an argument could be made that *Live Through This* was only significant because Kurt was dead).

Of course, that's only judging the quality of those albums in hindsight. The reality is that cornerstone groups were still releasing albums as late as 1997 (discounting Pearl Jam, of course, for reasons discussed in chapter 5). At the time, these albums seemed like noble attempts to evolve, but today those albums seem like cheap imitations of past glories or lazy attempts to cash in on the remains of grunge's cultural cachet. But even looking back on them, none of them were so bad that they could end a genre. Soundgarden's 1996 flop, *Down on the Upside*, was pretty disappointing, but it didn't make anybody rise up and revolt against the genre—it mostly just made people listen to their old copies of *Badmotorfinger* instead.

The breakup of Soundgarden actually seems like it should be a defining moment representing the end of a movement. They were one of the genre's oldest bands—the last surviving group from the *Deep Six* compilation way back in 1986—and their death would have made for a very poetic end to the revolution they helped birth over a decade prior. Unfortunately, much like many aspects of the movement, Soundgarden ended with a whimper instead of a bang. They were the sort of band that was so quiet and generally awkward in public together that they were constantly rumored to be breaking up, so the whisperings that their summer 1996 tour would be their last were not taken with any sort of seriousness (not to mention they were touring *Down on the Upside*, which seriously limited the number of people who were still paying attention). Following a show in Hawaii, the band quietly announced that they would play their last show two days later. For a group their size, it's in the running for the most anticlimatic breakup in history. So while it did mean the end for arguably the last forefather standing (again, discounting Pearl Jam), it didn't have a great deal of impact on the music world at large. News of the demise of Soundgarden was met mostly with shrugs.

So perhaps 1997 was too late; perhaps the genre had already ceased to exist by then. A strong argument can be made that grunge had officially ended in December of 1994, which was when Bush released their debut, *Sixteen Stone*. Bush is possibly the most maligned band in history: There was never a moment in their entire existence when they were granted the benefit of the doubt (except by the fifteen-year-old girls who went apeshit for front man Gavin Rossdale's hair). They were immediately accused of cashing checks over Kurt Cobain's corpse, and the fact that they played pitch-perfect simulacra of Nirvanaesque songs didn't help their case. Rossdale also did himself no favors by making arguments that while his band sounded a lot like Nirvana, Nirvana also ripped off the Pixies, which he felt was an axiom that somehow would make everything okay. All Rossdale ever wanted was to be in a successful band, but all people ever saw was an opportunist who had nailed down a minstrel act. *If this guy could do it,* rock fans thought, *what makes it special anymore?* People wanted to believe that grunge came from a place that was hard and visceral and *real.* Bush's four art students—*English* art students—had no relation to that place at all, yet "Little Things" is probably one of the best songs in the entire grunge canon. It's no wonder these guys took as much flak as they did.

But Gavin Rossdale did not bring about grunge's apocalypse—he was merely the first guy mistaken for a horseman. By the time Rossdale and company followed lockstep down the same path as Nirvana by hiring Steve Albini to produce the follow-up to their commercial smash, grunge's death rattle was only just beginning.

When Bush's Albini-produced *Razorblade Suitcase* (featuring singles such as "Swallowed" and "Greedy Fly" that no one ever wanted to admit were stunning), even the wannabes had flown the coop. Earlier that year, Stone Temple Pilots, one of the most hated bands of the 1990s, released *Tiny Music . . . Songs from the Vatican Gift Shop*, a tremendously odd collection of songs that saw the band experimenting with jazz-bo guitars and (huh?) lounge music. It was as illogical a musical step from 1994's *Purple* as was possible. *Purple* is perhaps the definitive statement of STP's musical ambition: They wanted to turn turgid sludge rock into streamlined, stadium-rock gold. They mostly succeeded, as every single song on *Purple* is an anthem, and they also dropped in "Interstate Love Song," a track that sounds like an Eagles outtake and is one of the best pieces of radio rock ever written. *Tiny Music* has basically no relation to its predecessor at all. Even the band that existed to do nothing but profit from grunge managed to be tired of it by '96.

But that still doesn't get us any closer to a definitive date of death for one of rock and roll's most maligned movements. In fact, even after the rats abandoned ship and Bush took over the airwaves, grunge still saw a little bit of a renaissance as late as 1998. That year, Pearl Jam released *Yield*, an album that is largely forgotten save for "Given to Fly," the band's last great radio hit (it's no mystery, either, as it openly cribs its melody from Led Zeppelin's "Going to California"). Unorthodox grunge-infused rockers Local H also saw success in '98 with the single "All the Kids Are Right." Grunge holdouts Live (who were sort of like a grunge U2), Silverchair (who were sort of like a grunge Skid Row), and Third Eye Blind (who were sort of terrible) were still dirtying up their guitars, distorting their vocals, and whining about their doomed lives.

Of course, these are horrible examples of latter-day grunge that have almost no connection to the bands that came out of Seattle nearly a decade prior. However, because those bands all had songs that were big as late as 1998 proves that the grunge *sound* was still de rigueur then. People had yet to become tired of it completely. The populace certainly preferred the watered-down version of the sound (hence the commercial and critical failure of Soundgarden's swan song, *Down on the Upside*, in '96), but they accepted a version of it nonetheless.

In fact, grunge soldiered on in one form or another for nearly another year after the last radio hits until it ran headfirst into one man and one man alone who crushed everything that grunge had stood for and finally, definitively, put it to bed. It would be poetic if that man were Axl Rose, the icon supposedly usurped by the flannel wearers years prior, the guy who choked on his magnum opus and disappeard underground, working on a mythical album called *Chinese Democracy*, which as of this writing still doesn't exist. It's a shame that Axl couldn't get it together in time to avenge himself. As it turned out, he did in fact put out a song under the Guns N' Roses name in 1999. Titled "Oh My God," it appeared on the sound track to the horrible Arnold Schwarzenegger versus Satan film *End of Days*. "Oh My God" was an appropriate title, as the end of that statement was typically "what the hell happened?" rather than "this is great!"

No, Axl cannot stand as the great grunge killer. Rather, the stake was driven through grunge's vampire heart by a far less assuming but still dangerous guy, a musician only in the loosest sense of the word, who probably didn't intend to destroy everything that was left of grunge but was probably cool with it, despite the tattoo of Kurt Cobain on his chest.

Of course, the great destroyer was Fred Durst. The band was Limp Bizkit. And grunge's last night on earth was Saturday night, July 24, 1999.

Woodstock '99 was a concept that was only slightly worse than that of Woodstock '94, which was one of the worst ideas of all time. In an effort to re-create the feel-good communal hippie vibe of the original Woodstock, some young promoters decided to overcharge college students to stay at understaffed and understocked camp-grounds while listening to mostly dog-terrible music for three days. Woodstock '94 was mostly harmless and notable only for the mud and how it affected the sets by Nine Inch Nails and Green Day, both of whom recalibrated people's perceptions by the end of their respective sets. Woodstock '94 was most certainly a boon-doggle, but a boondoggle in the "man, they didn't plan well for all this traffic" kind of way.

However, Woodstock '99 was a boondoggle in a "man, I sure hope I don't get beaten and raped" way. The 1999 version of the event will forever be remembered for the bonfires that burned un-controllably at the conclusion and for the accused sexual assaults that supposedly occurred in the mosh pits during several bands' sets. Though Red Hot Chili Peppers presided over the fires, the band that ushered in the greatest amount of destruction, both physically and metaphorically, was Limp Bizkit.

Hailing from Florida and led by the aforementioned Durst, Limp Bizkit was wildly popular during the summer of 1999. Their sopho-more album, *Significant Other*, was a massive success and stood on the shoulders of the hit singles "Nookie" and "Break Stuff." Durst himself was already becoming an icon, and his red baseball cap—usually worn backward—had become a symbol of adolescent rage, aggression, and hedonism. Unlike the grunge forefathers at the be-ginning of the decade, Durst didn't turn his rage inward, nor did he reflect on why he was angry. All he knew was that his life was unac-ceptable to him, and that was enough reason to stomp his feet, scream at the top of his lungs, and tear down the walls.

Limp Bizkit's albums (along with the rap-rock idiom entire) have aged even more poorly than the music from the grunge era. The main problem is twofold: Rap-rock doesn't operate very well as rap (most of the "MCs" were pretty leaden, though Durst's collaboration with Method Man and DJ Premier on "N 2 Gether Now" is relatively impressive), nor is it very good metal (most of "Break Stuff" sounds too polished and soft). Hanging on to those albums usually means either (1) you have a deep nostalgic attachment to the radio singles or (2) you are a member of Korn.

But back in July of '99, Fred Durst and Limp Bizkit were Kong huge, and their set at Woodstock brought out the savage in everyone. During "Break Stuff," fans started tearing apart large chunks of the fences and barriers around the stage. Fully embracing the moment, Durst decided to grab one of the broken planks and use it to crowd surf, creating one of the most memorable images of the entire festival. Of course, as this was going on, women were apparently being stripped and groped in the pit below.

Durst's joyride certainly was iconic, but it also represented a historical event that he likely didn't anticipate—it's the death of grunge. A white guy who thought himself to be hardcore encouraged legions to "break stuff" for no greater purpose other than to be noticed. In the same decade when Courtney Love bemoaned how little women are respected in the rock world, teenage rock fans decided just to do it all for the nookie. By the time Limp Bizkit's set at Woodstock '99 ended, Cobain had probably done several dozen rotations in his grave and Eddie Vedder likely cried a single tear, because Armageddon had finally arrived for the attitude and ideology that they inadvertently had created eight years prior. The dam had been cracked for some time, but Durst hit the plunger on the dynamite, and the deluge overwhelmed everyone. Rap-rock was in fashion, and nobody cared why anybody was upset anymore. The point was that they were upset, and the rest of the universe had to acknowledge that or pay the consequences.

Self-reflection and irony made way for the new whiners, and these guys were out for blood.

With grunge dead, rock music splintered in a million different directions, and the end of the millennium saw no single significant genre rise above the rest to dictate the style and substance of everybody else. Rap-rock soldiered on and quickly evolved into nü metal, an angsty variation that combined the attitude of rap-rock with the big hooks of hair metal and the extra sludge of a genre that had become quite familiar to many of the twentysomethings who were forming these bands.

Indeed, even as early as 2000, rock music already started to look awfully familiar. One of the biggest hits of the summer of 2000 was "Higher," by Christ-loving arena metallers Creed. Not only did buff front man Scott Stapp sound like he was channeling Eddie Vedder (as countless rock singers had done since 1991), but the chorus sounded an awful lot like "Alive," except rather than tell his story, Scott was asking Jesus to give him a hand. Less than a year had gone by since Fred Durst killed grunge off, and already it was coming back around again. But like any walking dead, something was off, and what was left happened to retain the absolute worst aspects of grunge without the things that offset it, and guitar-based music has yet to recover in an acceptable fashion. People have been declaring rock dead for so long now that nobody noticed when it actually happened. Music journalists have been crying wolf for years, but now all the sheep are dead. Durst broke the fence, Stapp hauled away the carcasses, and rock fans have been left behind, the lonely shepherds searching in vain for a purpose.

THE GROUP of loud guitar-based bands that found success at the turn of the millennium—Creed, Nickelback, Puddle of Mudd, and others—represents the absolute nadir of rock and roll, and grunge is partially to blame. A twenty-five-year-old front man of a rock band in 2001 was fifteen when *Ten* became a massive hit, so it's only natural that bands such as Pearl Jam, Soundgarden, and Alice in Chains served as these groups' inspiration and the basis for their musical development. Unfortunately, they took the sonic sludge and divorced it from the humor and the self-reflection. What they (and music fans) were left with was a formula for dull, plodding, middle-of-the-road guitar rock that has not only driven music into the ground but also hurt the legacy of grunge.

Of course, the legacy would have been in doubt anyway. As has been discussed elsewhere in this volume, even the most classic records from the early nineties have not aged well, and the individual singles mostly show off what was stereotypical about the genre. Soundgarden's "Black Hole Sun" still sounds like an amazing metal tune, mostly because it is, but despite its Beatles-esque melody, it still feels like it's much longer than it actually is. It's not the kind of heavy that makes it feel intense and awesome—rather, it's the kind of heavy that is exhausting. Same goes for Pearl Jam's "Alive." When it's heard today, only the die-hard fans are able to recount the story told in the lyrics, while everyone else hears Eddie Vedder contorting his blustery baritone around a chugging riff. Again, it still sounds incredible, but after fifteen years it represents something that is less than credible. The rise of the second wave of Pearl Jam clones certainly magnified that tunnel-vision effect, but that is the natural order of big songs. Even legendary tunes are mostly only remembered for one thing: "Stairway to Heaven" is generally remembered as either (1) a really long song, or (2) a really long song with a really crazy-ass guitar solo. "Like a Rolling Stone" will forever be identified as the song that Dylan used to go electric, which was probably a convenient development for him because it saved that track from being remembered as one of the many Dylan songs that don't make any sense. History has a way of distilling pop songs down to a singular essence, and grunge's flameout, combined with the bands it begat, has made history a very cruel mistress indeed.

AT THE beginning of this volume, the rise of grunge and the end of rock and roll were pinned on one man and one man alone: Axl Rose. Axl's miscues with the *Use Your Illusion* albums put the final nail in the coffin of eighties metal and set in motion the chain re-action that led to legions of people dressing like truckers and sup-porting bands such as the Fastbacks. But there is a reason that Axl is still around, and that Mötley Crüe can have a massively success-ful reunion tour, and that Van Halen is still largely considered to be damn close to the greatest band of all time, and it's something that both the grunge granddaddies and their scions could have used to stave off obsolescence and save rock music.

Sex.

The harsh truth is this: All great rock-and-roll songs are about sex, or at least make you think about sex. Bands such as the Rolling Stones, Led Zeppelin, and Van Halen were all exceptional for a va-riety of different reasons, but the one thing they had in common was that they constantly encouraged their audience to think about fucking *all the time.* Even if it didn't seem like a song was about sex, those bands still played those songs as though they were try-ing to get laid. Call it what you will—the attitude, the swagger—but those bands owned it, and if there's one great legacy that hair metal left behind, it's that just about every one of those bands (with du-bious exceptions like Stryper) understood that fundamental fact. It's a basic idea that you can build upon—once you've got your groove covered, you can move on to actually write a song about sex (like "Hot for Teacher"), or you can write a song about Satan ("Sympathy for the Devil"), or you can write a song about *Lord of the Rings* ("The Battle of Evermore"). It's the idea that absolutely cripples ideologues. It's the reason that prog rock is so incredily lame. While a lot of prog (like Rush) sounds like traditional metal, the aesthetic is all about technical mastery and innovation. Songs about math don't get you laid, as any high school band geek can admit.

Grunge (and its aftermath) was similarly crippled by the lack of sex. Most grunge rockers were so wound up in the idea of sounding *important* that they didn't bother to attempt the swagger. Grunge was about salvation, not fornication.

Scanning the back catalog of various bands, it's hard to find grunge tunes that inspire any unlawful carnal knowledge. Stone Temple Pilots had a song on their debut called "Sex Type Thing," but that was about getting into the mind of an aggressor and was more creepy than sexy. The closest thing Soundgarden came to sex was "Spoonman," but that song is derailed by the fact that it's likely about heroin, one of the only drugs that don't inspire you to get laid (the fact that the video featured four minutes of a guy playing the spoons didn't help, either). Nirvana's "Heart-Shaped Box" has a sinister sexiness to it, but it's negated by Kurt's lyrics about eating cancer and throwing down umbilical nooses. The whole oeuvre is a sexual desert—there's nary a pelvic thrust in sight.

Of course, the lack of sex in grunge was beyond logical, as there were a lot of mitigating factors that worked against the natural inclination to shake one's ass. For one thing, the grungies dressed like truckers, paid little attention to personal hygiene, and mumbled a lot—these were not guys who were making any sort of attempt to attract the opposite sex (at least by traditional means). Think what you want about the guys in hair metal bands, but those guys knew how to keep themselves together. In fact, they were so primped and preened that they usually looked like women (except in the case of Twisted Sister's Dee Snider, who legitimately intended to look like a woman—albeit the most hideous woman this side of Golda Meir).

Not unlike the pimple-faced nerd who can't get a date and made it a point to shun women, the grunge community's take on carnal affairs was something of a holier-than-thou stance. Since sex was such a big part of eighties metal (and such a massive topic in the greater annals of rock history), grunge rockers simply added it to the pile of things to shun because they were somehow greater. Besides, they were so busy wrapped up in their own heads that they found no time to embrace the fairer sex (at least from a song-writing perspective). A lot of this attitude likely came as part of the genrewide "respect for women" soapbox, mostly given legs by Cobain, who was constantly endorsing the musical and philosophical prowess of riot grrrl bands and taking a vocal stand against domestic abuse (or at least vocal enough for people to call him a hypocrite when police were called to his home on a domestic disturbance call in 1993). In fact, one of the best compilations of nineties alternative rock was called *Home Alive: The Art of Self-Defense*, a charity album that featured Nirvana, Hole, Pearl Jam, and Soundgarden and benefited a Seattle-based nonprofit organization that provides self-defense classes and violence prevention education. Since grunge mixed with riot grrrl sonically and geographically (both had their roots in the Pacific Northwest), it was only natural that they mixed philosophically as well.

As a consequence, the great grunge seduction song never existed; it remains a mystery what exactly teens and twentysomethings were listening to while knocking the boots circa 1992. Perhaps that's why Candlebox got so popular—they were writing the grunge equivalent of eighties power ballads. Your older brother was able to make out to "Every Rose Has Its Thorn," but the best you could muster was "Far Behind."

Unfortunately for the bands that weren't Candlebox, sex is an eternal musical trope, and not delving into it cost everybody a lot of longevity (including Candlebox, who were ultimately dealt the same fate). Personal pain doesn't stick in the minds of listeners except under extreme circumstances (or attached to a huge hook; see "Alive"), and political beliefs fade with fashion (ever think about what all the anti-Bush songs will sound like ten years down the line?). There is a reason that the cliché is "sex, drugs, and rock 'n' roll." All the good Mötley Crüe songs are about chasing down strippers, hookers, midwestern virgins, and various other objects of lust ("Too Fast for Love," "Girls Girls Girls") or about getting so unbelievably wasted that all of life seems utterly transcendent ("Dr. Feelgood"), and the best songs are about both ("Livewire," "Kickstart My Heart").

Of course, grunge rockers sang about drugs and death all the time (in fact, they very much recognized that the former sometimes led to the latter, in the case of Andrew Wood and later Layne Staley). But the bands had a hard time making it sound *cool.* Whenever Alice in Chains sang about getting high, as they did for the length of their best album, *Dirt,* it never sounded awesome—it just sounded frightening. Though heroin came in vogue (see chapter 6), it is doubtful that reasonable people started shooting up because they heard Kurt did it. Listening to Van Halen and then getting drunk makes perfect logical sense, as everybody wanted to have half as much fun as David Lee Roth seemed to be having all the time. As far as most people were concerned, doing heroin meant sitting at home, locked away with your own thoughts, desperately warding off dementia, and probably vomiting uncontrollably. Save for the characters in Irvine Welsh's *Trainspotting,* nobody has ever found that cool.

Which of course is the main problem. Rock music is supposed to be cool. It's supposed to dictate a lifestyle where pleasure is at its maximum. Grunge was cool, but it wasn't any sort of cool that anybody was used to; it wasn't "traditional cool." All rock stars re-

ally need to do is follow the coolness model that was set up decades ago by James Dean: They need to be aloof, they need to
seem dangerous, and they need to wear extremely tight pants.
Grunge was mainstream for a time and that made it cool, but it
wasn't the sort of cool that lasts—it was "freak cool." Every once in
a while (typically once per generation), something bubbles up from
under and becomes part of an otherwise normal zeitgeist. For example, disco was a quiet pocket of coked-up clubheads who happened to stumble upon a half decade of relevance, only to see
their music, clothes, and language fade into parody. Grunge did a
similar thing—the legions got so big and so loud that the mainstream couldn't suppress it anymore, but like any counterculture
worth its sand, it was quickly co-opted and sold back to the kids
who invented it. The image that grunge projected had little to do
with what was traditionally defined as cool, and though trend spot-
ters like to claim that the concept of cool is constantly evolving,
that's actually a lie. It's just the same concept, recycled over and
over again. Fashion changes, but philosophy stays the same. And
just like disco, whose songs were mostly about dancing (and sometimes even *specific* dances), grunge's themes simply were not time-
less enough. Of course we should always remain diligent about
domestic abuse, horrible childhoods, and post-traumatic stress disorder, but keeping those types of things in the public conciousness
is actually more difficult than keeping a single there.

Grunge was also missing its living embodiments of cool. As a
good example, take Eddie Vedder. Eddie could have very easily
been cool, and when Pearl Jam first debuted it looked like Vedder
was going to be the grunge James Dean: He was dark, he brooded
a lot, and he kept his personal life a mysterious secret. Unfortunately, he decided to try to parlay his band's popularity into something practical (a sure sign of overthinking, and overthinking is not
cool). The real nail in his cool coffin was the assault on Ticketmas-

ter. Cool people don't like authority, but they never take on "the man" directly—they simply ignore the authority and find a way to live outside the law (as Pearl Jam did on their Fall 1995 tour, which saw them play only non-Ticketmaster venues). But Eddie kept talking, and we started to learn more, and eventually he seemed totally harmless. The harmless are not cool. Clearly, Eddie has been modeling his career after Neil Young, who was never cool when he was supposed to matter (though is cool now in a sort of "man, my crazy uncle is awesome" kind of way—perhaps Eddie will evolve into that, though he may need to release an ill-advised new wave album first). Timelessness has been grunge's enemy, and the lack of truly cool icons has certainly contributed to the rift between the music's popularity and its place in history.

SO WHERE does that leave us today? In the spring of 2006, Pearl Jam put out their best album since *Vitalogy*, but it was treated just like any other Pearl Jam album: obsessed over by the diehards and largely ignored by the populace at large. Mudhoney also released an album in 2006 to little fanfare. The rest of the grunge breakout bands (Nirvana, Soundgarden, and Alice in Chains) had been long broken up, though Alice in Chains did tour in the spring of 2006 with Call of the Wild singer William DuVall taking the deceased Layne Staley's place on lead vocals.

Even the bands that were not necessarily grunge bands but still got a good rub from the popularity of it were finding it difficult. Billy Corgan put out a weak-selling solo album in 2005 and kept saying that he wants to get the Smashing Pumpkins back together, even though it is assumed that the reunited version of the Pumpkins would include neither guitarist James Iha nor original bass player D'Arcy Wretzky. Elsewhere, Stone Temple Pilots called it quits several years ago, and Weiland went on to front the Guns N' Roses retirement band Velvet Revolver, which in Weiland's case was the most logical move he could make—with all the drug arrests and bombast, he's always been more hair metal than anything else. Even Beck, who bore no sonic resemblance to any of the other bands and yet was lumped in often because of his scraggly looks and his "slacker" attitude, had a hard time finding a break. His 2005 album, *Guero*, sold 1 million, but he seemed to be spinning the wheels a bit, as *Guero* did sound an awful lot like a rehash of his breakout 1996 album, *Odelay*.

The one guy who seems to have maintained some sort of cultural importance is Chris Cornell, the broody, big-voiced former front man of Soundgarden who joined up with three-quarters of Rage Against the Machine to form Audioslave. Both of Audioslave's first two albums—their 2002 self-titled debut and their 2005 follow-up, *Out of Exile*—went platinum with a good old-fashioned slow-burn approach. The typical model for a big-ticket album release is to score a big opening week and then hope the subsequent singles can keep the album afloat; otherwise it slowly sinks off the Billboard charts (this is the same model Hollywood uses for big-budget movies). Audioslave never broke out over-the-top, but both of those albums stuck around the middle portions of the charts, selling consistently as the singles became AOR radio staples. (Their third, 2005's *Revelations*, sputtered.)

Though it seems like Audioslave has found the solution, they are actually a big part of the problem. Stylistically, neither of their records is as flashy or as interesting as either Soundgarden or Rage Against the Machine was. It's little more than hearty meat-and-potatoes rock. That's not necessarily a negative, but it does put Audioslave in some dubious company.

What other bands dominate AOR radio, the last form of rock

radio left in the United States? It's the grunge bastard children: Nickelback, Puddle of Mudd, Creed, and every other band that appropriated the grunge sound at the turn of the millennium.

There will always be a need for guitar-based music. Rock has had many permutations during its life span and has been declared "dead" more often than Kenny on *South Park.* The "indie rock revolution," which was supposed to set the world on fire with the Strokes' debut album in 2001, never got off the ground commercially. The postmodern prog of System of a Down and Mars Volta has been successful but still seems like more of an insular niche product (even though they sell hundreds of thousands of records, neither band really has the desire to make a crossover attempt).

But until bands, record labels, and rock fans divorce themselves from the idea that grunge can happen again, rock and roll will continue to be unsatisfying. People still talk about finding "the next Nirvana." They aren't actually looking for a band that sounds like Nirvana, but they want a band that will come out of the underground and change everything. But because of the information-overload age in which we live, those sudden discoveries are now impossible. Bands are no longer capable of bubbling up from under. Rock fans are so sensitive to hype that they are already burned out before a band has a chance to release its debut. Take the Arctic Monkeys, for example. They were hyped on the Internet as the next big thing, christened geniuses by the British press, and created an unbelievable fervor about their debut. But the information was processed so quickly and intensely that by the time their album was actually available, people had become sick of them. The grunge revolution happened organically, and until we stop trying to *induce* a revolution, rock music could be in this doldrum state for quite a long time.

If only Axl hadn't messed up *Use Your Illusion.*

—

APPENDIX

The Great Grunge Discography

IT'S TRUE THAT HISTORY HAS NOT BEEN KIND TO MANY OF THE bands from the nineties that carried the banner of alt rock. The albums put out under the grunge header made much more of an impact on a sociological level than on a musical level, so setting the parameters for the relative importance or impact of any particular album is difficult. The normal rules for rock albums simply don't apply.

Choosing the best rock records ever made is relatively easy. Typically, some combination of popularity and level of influence helps to determine whether or not a rock album is worth remembering. This is why almost every Beatles and Led Zeppelin album can be considered an all-time great, as those albums were both incredibly commercially successful and copied by an incredible variety of other groups (which still continues today). Grunge albums are a tougher nut to crack: Only a handful of albums had the kind of wild commercial success that makes true legends, and there were very few albums that had the sort of influence that helps minor records transcend the exposure barrier. For example, while Pavement's *Slanted and Enchanted* still has yet to go gold, it's agreed that it is a great record because of its far-reaching sphere of influence on several aesthetic levels.

Most grunge albums lacked that middle ground—they were either runaway hits with no substance (like most of the catalog of Stone Temple Pilots) or artistically committed albums that nobody cared about (like most everything Mudhoney ever put out).

That being said, the following albums are not necessarily records that need to be kept precious for future generations. They are simply the best representations of the grunge era. Many of these barely existed outside of their immediate context, but therein lie the details of the story of grunge. The broad strokes are taken care of by the huge releases, but the tiny, forgotten notes are handled by the albums that fell into the margins, were critically dismissed, or were entirely misunderstood. In fact, the vast majority of the albums on this list are by bands that were absolutely slammed by critics, at least at first. The grunge era was a time for extremely vitriolic rock criticism, because for a time it seemed like all writers had to do was scream loud enough and suddenly their favorite bands would get noticed. Conversely, critics wanted to work hard at suppressing things that they deemed worthless. Ironically, a bunch of those bands and albums initially dismissed by critics at large ended up becoming legendary, or at least are the things still remembered from that era.

So here are the most necessary selections for constructing the musical representation of what it was like to be a grunge fan in the early nineties. It should be duly noted that the criteria for inclusion on this list are relatively loose; sonically, at least, there is a great deal of discrepancy between many of these releases (which only makes sense, as there is barely any uniting line between Nirvana, Pearl Jam, and Soundgarden, outside of the fact that they were all from Seattle). The selections are in order of importance, from lesser to greater, as decided by a very complicated scientific process involving many beakers of blue bubbling liquid.

THE VERVE PIPE, *Villains* (RCA, 1996): This is a perfect example of the alt-rock mentality run amok. When dirty-sounding bands started getting on the radio, the natural reaction was to make *all* songs sound a little dirty, which is why there was a glut of bands that had excellent songs but were presented as wannabes or post-grunge hangers-on and given short shrift. The Verve Pipe was one of those bands. Front man and songwriter Brian Vander Ark is an incredible crafter of tunes (in addition to having an overly complicated name—science has yet to prove whether or not these two phenomena are related). When the Verve Pipe made their major-label debut, they were paired with producer Jerry Harrison, the former Talking Heads member who had produced a great many alternative-sounding albums for bands such as Live and had curated the ultra-alt *Empire Records* sound track. The result became Vander Ark's catchy songs dressed in shabby T-shirts and presented in slacker fashion.

The song that everybody will always remember from *Villains* is "The Freshmen," a dopey ballad about regretting things you did in college and the death of innocence. It's acceptable, but the rockers on *Villains* are far more convincing, like the moody "Photograph" (which has a great organ line that gives it a slightly creepy funhouse feel) and the blustery "Cup of Tea." The Verve Pipe will forever be remembered as simply a one-hit wonder, and their album makes it onto this list mostly as an example of the type of crowbarring that many bands faced in the grunge and postgrunge eras. A couple of months after *Villains* was released, Matchbox 20 came along and essentially put out the exact same album and usurped

Villains' audience, but Matchbox front man Rob Thomas always seemed like a douche bag, so Vander Ark's forgotten opus gets the nod.

GIN BLOSSOMS, *New Miserable Experience* (A&M, 1992): When hip-hop began to slowly take over the pop airwaves later in the nineties (spearheaded largely by the success of P. Diddy and his ilk), the sonics of rap music began to bleed into other genres on the pop landscape. For a while, it seemed like you couldn't turn on a radio without hearing a bit of hip-hop influence in just about everything (except maybe in country music; the whole "hick-hop" movement didn't start until a decade later). Pop groups suddenly employed tough break beats, and the genre known as "rap-rock" or "rap-metal" bubbled up from under with the success of bands such as Limp Bizkit.

Though grunge didn't have the same kind of staying power as hip-hop has proven to have, it did influence the greater pop landscape in very profound and immediate ways. As with the Verve Pipe, Gin Blossoms was simply a pop band that had an excellent songwriter at the helm. All it took was a little dirtying up of their guitars and a handful of angsty-sounding vocals and suddenly they became "edgy." By today's standards, *New Miserable Experience* is the sort of milquetoast album that your mom likes listening to when she wants to get a little crazy. Actually, it sounded sort of wussy even in 1992, but the songs were so catchy that nobody seemed to notice. Gin Blossoms was so huge but burned out so quickly that the track listing on their debut reads a lot like a greatest hits compilation: "Until I Fall Away," "Hey Jealousy," "Mrs. Rita," and "Found Out About You" are all pop gems that well outlasted their time in the sun (it seems like "Hey Jealousy" will never, ever die). If Gin Blossoms' music wasn't that intense, their biography was: Their main songwriter and original guiding force killed himself after being kicked out of the band for his alcohol problem, seemingly right at the peak of *New Miserable Experience*'s exposure. It's the sort of story that can make a bunch of boring white guys seem really *heavy*. All their songs seemed to be sad, and since all those guys in flannel were sad all the time, too, being forlorn suddenly made you "alternative." It doesn't take much to fool pop music audiences, really.

Gin Blossoms should not be remembered as a grunge band (or an indie band or even a *good* band), but without the power of alt rock ruling the radio, they probably would have remained simply another bar band from the desert who happened to dress like convenience store clerks.

PRIMUS, *Sailing the Seas of Cheese* (Interscope, 1991): **One of the big reasons people get nostalgic for the early nineties is because it seemed like such an open-ended time, when just about anything and anybody could be a breakout hit. Primus is a prime example of that attitude. When they first came along in 1990, nobody knew what the fuck Primus was, or how they should be listened to, or what to do with them. When** *Sailing the Seas of Cheese* **came out and "Jerry Was a Race Car Driver" became an MTV hit, nobody had the energy to come up with a genre for them, so they were thrown in the "alternative" bin, even though they sounded like a supercaffeinated car crash between Frank Zappa and Yngwie Malmsteen, two guys rarely mentioned as grunge influences. Fifteen years later, people** *still* **don't know what the fuck to do with Primus (or with any of front man and bass virtuoso Les Claypool's many side collaborations and solo projects), but the recognition and success of** *Sailing the Seas of Cheese* **proved that 1991 was a great year to be a band that nobody understood.**

Musically, *Sailing the Seas of Cheese* **is not Primus's most accessible work (that would be 1993's** *Pork Soda***), nor does it have the**

most accomplished songs (1995's *Tales from the Punchbowl* takes that crown), but it does offer a complete picture of what Primus represents, which is to say aggressively complex bass riffs offset by jagged guitar squeals and Claypool's sorta-dark, sorta-goofy sense of humor. "Jerry Was a Race Car Driver" had an off-kilter storytelling quality that perfectly complemented the band's visual sense (in reality, the video for the song was probably more popular than the song itself), and "Those Damned Blue Collar Tweakers" does exploit the quiet verse/loud chorus dynamic that was so prevalent among the alternative-rock scene. It's a difficult listen and sounds pretty dated today, but it's an amazing artifact that acts as a representation of just how adventurous and/or confused listeners (and MTV) were circa 1991.

BUFFALO TOM, *Big Red Letter Day* (Beggars Banquet, 1993): Boston has always been a weird town for rock and roll. Aerosmith and the Cars are both from Beantown, but there never seemed to be anything definitively *Bostonian* about Steven Tyler and his band of merry men or Ric Ocasek's crew (they never sang about the Red Sox or referenced the chowder at Legal Seafood, for example). When grunge hit, the Boston scene got a little recognition because there happened to be a lot of bands in the city at the time that were playing vaguely "alternative" music, but there was never really a definitive Boston band that scored big during the alt-rock heyday. In fact, the band that got the most success during the alternative era was the Mighty Mighty Bosstones, who were a goddamn *ska band.* Though one of grunge's forefathers came from Boston in the form of the Pixies, no Boston band broke through the way the bands from Seattle, Los Angeles, and Chicago did.

Of course, there were plenty of also-rans that enjoyed smallish careers making excellent songs for a devoted audience. Buffalo

Tom began as a noisy Replacementesque sorta-punk band, but eventually their sound evolved into a very mature-sounding rootsy alt rock that would later inform breakout acts such as Counting Crows and the Wallflowers.

Big Red Letter Day is sort of a transition album from their former selves to what they would become. Their previous effort, *Let Me Come Over*, is arguably the better album (and was more popular); this record contains the finest moment in Buffalo Tom history and is the reason that they will be remembered by pop culture historians. In what was probably their largest bit of exposure in the United States (they were always much larger in Europe, a trait they shared with many grunge bands), the group guested on an episode of *My So-Called Life*, a moody show about a teenage girl named Angela Chase and her many moods. Critically adored but unloved by the TV-watching masses, *My So-Called Life* became a massive cult hit and probably offers the most accurate representation of what it was like to be a teenager in the early nineties. In the show's best episode, Angela (played by Claire Danes) is jilted publicly by her crush Jordan Catalano (Jared Leto) at a Buffalo Tom concert. However, the next day at school Jordan makes the save by holding hands with Angela, representing the first time he's publicly displayed his affection for her. The song that underscores that entire sequence is Buffalo Tom's "Late at Night," a gorgeously lilting, melancholy ballad from *Big Red Letter Day* made immortal by its inclusion on *My So-Called Life*. By itself, it's simply a great song, but when paired with such an incredibly important moment in the grunge zeitgeist, it became totally transcendent.

EVERCLEAR, *Sparkle and Fade* (Capitol, 1995): It's sort of amazing that Everclear didn't break out until 1995, when this album was released, as front man Art Alexakis had a perfect grunge pedigree: He was from the Pacific Northwest (Portland), he was a recovering junkie, and his band played shambling, angst-ridden punk songs that owed as much to the Replacements as they did to the Sex Pistols. Still, the formula didn't break out until '95, when "Santa Monica" became a huge radio hit. The career trajectory of Everclear got very strange after this album, as Alexakis decided to make his whole catalog into midtempo rocks songs that recalled seventies AM radio hits (going as far as writing a song called "AM Radio"). But *Sparkle and Fade* has everything a good post-Cobain alternative album needed: a big single (the aforementioned "Santa Monica"), a conscientious rocker ("Heartspark Dollarsign," a song about a white guy dating a black girl), and a lot of songs about drugs ("Heroin Girl," "Electra Made Me Blind," "Strawberry"). Alexakis also had a world-weariness about him that was palpable, which was probably due to the fact that he was already thirty-three years old and was married with a daughter by the time his band finally started being successful. Even the title suggested a knowing wink to the fleetingness of fame–a theme that continued, as the follow-up was titled *So Much for the Afterglow.* By grunge standards, Alexakis was grandfatherly by the time he got famous, and he fully embraced his role as alt-rock elder statesman. *Sparkle and Fade* remains his most raw and most definitive contribution to the rock landscape.

LIVE, *Throwing Copper* (Radioactive, 1994): It's lazy to simply call Live "the alt-rock U2," a moniker that chased them since their debut and only disappeared after the band became irrelevant (any avoidance of shark jumping was officially put to bed by front man Ed Kowalczyk's appearance on *American Idol* in the spring of 2006). But there is no greater moniker, as Kowalczyk is just as preachy as Bono and the band's devotion to spirituality greatly informs their arena-ready rock tunes. Though they got a bit of attention for their debut, *Mental Jewelry*, this sophomore record represents Live at the height of their powers. Kowalczyk wails like a grungy preacher while the band pulsates and explodes behind him, leaving mostly a fine white ash. Released during an era when self-importance was not only encouraged but also sometimes required, Live was the sort of band that teenagers always thought was profound—and perhaps they would be if they didn't constantly remind us how profound they actually were.

Still, if you can get past Kowalczyk's heavy-handedness and enjoy these songs as overpowering stadium anthems, *Throwing Copper* is a pretty excellent album, and even the baldfaced pretense is at least *interesting*. Live used the quiet verse/loud chorus dynamic as well as anybody, as shown in "Selling the Drama," "All Over You," and "I Alone." It's a testament to the power of the band's melodies when Kowalczyk can sing a lyric like "The beauty of this vision alone just like yesterday's sunset has been perverted by the sentimental and mistaken for love" (on "Iris") and it still somehow sounds like a pretty awesome rock song.

Most of Live's crossover success came from the ballad "Lightning Crashes," a song about the cycle of life that actually contains the lyric "Her placenta falls to the floor." It was always the slow song that grunge kids requested at middle school dances, which was strange because just like Pearl Jam's "Black"(the other most requested grunge ballad at sock hops), you absolutely cannot dance to it, in any capacity, at all. Plus, there's a line about a *placenta*, for chrissakes. Not even Bono ever sang about that. Still, *Throwing Copper* remains an important and influential album, because it was one of the last times a band was this brainy and also this loud and this popular. It's since been an elusive combination.

LOVE BATTERY, *Dayglo* (Sub Pop, 1992): Not a whole lot of people have heard of Love Battery, but it is one of those bands that always get mentioned when you talk to people who were in Seattle during the grunge explosion. Love Battery got absolutely no love outside of the confines of their home city, but inside the Seattle clubs they were treated like the Second Coming. It's no mystery as to why, as Love Battery was made up of members of other well-respected bands in the area that were considered seminal (most notably the U-Men and Skin Yard), making them the least illustrious supergroup in the history of rock and roll. They must have been the most logical signing Sub Pop ever made.

Honestly, it's surprising that Love Battery didn't break out at least a little bit, as this, their second and best full-length, is a roundly excellent introduction that well utilizes the psychedelic elements among the noisy McCartney-meets-stoner-rock riffs and melodies. The songs (especially the opening triptych of "Out of Focus," "Foot," and "Damaged") have a lovely, delirious, churning quality, as though the guys from Pearl Jam suddenly got really into the "Norwegian Wood"–era Beatles. This sort of grunge-cum-psych-cum-roots sound was done much better by Screaming Trees, and in all honesty the record loses a bit of momentum toward the end, veering off into druggy noise a little too easily. But the bottom line is that *everybody* who ever hung out with a bunch of bearded guys at the Crocodile Club swore by Love Battery, and that's why it makes this list. The songs are pretty good, but its reputation carries it.

GREEN RIVER, *Come On Down* (Homestead, 1985): Arguably the first real "grunge" album, *Come On Down* falls behind 1987's *Dry as a Bone* as far as sonic quality goes, but these songs are a fascinating study in two worlds being pulled apart in one band. On one side were Mark Arm and Steve Turner's crazed, noise-centric, wailing songs about restlessness. On the other side were the riff-based seventies rock influences of Stone Gossard and Jeff Ament. Since

Arm is the front man and handles the singing and is the only band member with writing credits on all the tracks on *Come On Down*, it ends up sounding a lot like the early Mudhoney recordings, albeit with a little more metal influence (mostly due to Ament's very metal-sounding bass playing—it's low and thick and always seems to want to pull the songs into a groove, which Turner's guitar constantly resists).

"Swallow My Pride" is the best track on this album, and it also ended up being Green River's only minor "hit," at least within the confines of the early Seattle scene (Pearl Jam occasionally drops it into their live sets, and it's often the track dusted off for Green River "reunions," whenever PJ and Mudhoney tour together). On it, Arm moans, "This ain't the Summer of Love," and that lyric not only predicted a pattern of lyricism for the next decade, but also predicted an overall attitude toward everything, because (1) that is a completely hopeless line in the sense that it predicts misery in the face of assumed utopia, (2) it represents a longing for days gone by, at least one of which we can *never* know as a people, (3) it references Blue Oyster Cult, which fulfills the need to pay homage to the seventies, and (4) that reference might be a completely ironic mention or an in-joke between Mark Arm and one of the dudes from the Melvins (and it's impossible to tell exactly). Arm managed to give birth to the mentality of every twentysomething man (and most twentysomething women) for more than ten years—it's a shame he was never able to capitalize on it. *Come On Down* remains necessary because it's a good starting point for the rest of the scene (though the next definitive album wouldn't appear until Soundgarden dropped *Ultramega OK* almost three years later) and because it laid the groundwork that all the bands after it stayed surprisingly loyal to. Of course, most of the bands that followed actually contained former members of Green River, so perhaps they were just spreading the disease by acting like themselves. In any event, it's still a pretty great record.

REALITY BITES *sound track* (RCA, 1994): It should be duly noted that this is absolutely, positively *not* a grunge album in any capacity. In fact, it's not even an alt-rock record, an alt-pop album, or an example of any of the other odd monikers used to qualify sounds that people really didn't understand circa 1994. Again, its vitality isn't so much defined by the songs included on it but by what those songs represent, as it highlights a number of odd sociological occurrences. *Reality Bites* was a mostly uninteresting romantic comedy (just like *Singles*!) that accidentally became a cultural touchstone (again, like *Singles*). In spite of its insipidness, it got a lot of things right: Ben Stiller's square music exec was a perfect grunge-era villain, Ethan Hawke's moody hipster represented the tortured artist/slacker to a T, and it starred Janeane Garofalo. Moving forward, the movie will be represented more for its sound track, and rightfully so, because it takes a whole bunch of songs that have almost no relationship to one another and creates an "alternative" mix tape that makes no sense and every kind of sense simultaneously. It's got a bunch of bands that could actually be considered alternative, such as Dinosaur Jr., the Juliana Hatfield 3, and the Posies, a handful of artists who probably *seemed* alternative but turned out to be lame (all eyes are on you, Lenny Kravitz), and a bunch of seemingly throwaway tracks that don't seem to have anything to do with anything. (What was World Party doing there? What the hell is Me Phi Me?) But that level of eclecticism (and the willingness to have an "anything goes" attitude) is wholly emblematic of rock fans in the nineties. The perception is that the grunge era was actually a very narrow time for music because fans were using an indie-kid mentality to judge music. In all actuality, it opened up doors for a lot of bands not necessarily because they were great but because people were desperate to stay on the cutting edge. Suddenly, knowing about a band before anybody else meant something on a pretty large scale. People who are serious about rock music have always felt that way, but in the nineties the mainstream wanted to feel that way. It led to a lot of false positives, but it also kept people's minds open (for a short time, at least).

The sound track to *Reality Bites* will forever be known as the launching point for the career of Lisa Loeb, whose song "Stay" went to number one before she even had a record contract. "Stay" remains an excellent little slice of folk-pop, but her greatest contribution will forever be the video for "Stay," where she wanders through an apartment, sings to a cat, and wears those sexy librarian glasses that became the accessory that still drives Ethan Hawke–esque guys wild. In that one three-minute clip, Loeb became a grunge sex symbol–consider her the alt-rock Tawny Kitaen (though Lisa has never knowingly humped a car).

STONE TEMPLE PILOTS, *Purple* (Atlantic, 1994): Was there ever a band as hated as Stone Temple Pilots? A better question: Was there ever a band that was as hated and more or less deserved it as Stone Temple Pilots? When they first showed up in 1992, everything about them seemed contrived: Weiland sounded just like Eddie Vedder, their breakout single, "Plush," seemed like a b side from *Vs.*, and STP was from Southern California, home of Mötley Crüe, Guns N' Roses, and the majority of the trashy bands that grunge was supposedly killing off. Weiland even tried to diffuse some controversy about misogyny (the song "Sex Type Thing" was considered sexist) by wearing a dress, a practice that Kurt Cobain was a fan of. There didn't seem to be anything genuine about the guys from Los Angeles who sounded like Pearl Jam and looked a little too rock-and-roll to really be alternative.

Then a funny thing happened on the way to Stone Temple Pilots' up-and-down career: They made a great album. 1994's *Purple*, released only a handful of weeks after Cobain's suicide, managed to bridge the same gap between grunge, metal, and stadium rock as Soundgarden did, and STP even managed to do it more artfully. The opening dirge, "Meat Plow," has an amazingly heavy low end, and while Weiland does channel Alice in Chains' Layne Staley a little too acutely, it's still an excellent little rock song. Weiland does manage to find his own voice on the best parts of *Purple*, namely on the massive hit "Interstate Love Song," which is the best track of the entire grunge era not called "Smells Like Teen Spirit" (and since "Smells Like Teen Spirit" is less a song than a cultural milestone, STP sneaks into number one). "Interstate Love Song" sounds like exactly what it feels like to drive down the highway in California, and if there's a sentiment that is any less grunge than that, it would be remarkable.

Elsewhere, there are hints of psychedelia ("Lounge Fly," "Vasoline") that would be explored more thoroughly on later albums with mixed results. Weiland also revealed himself to be grunge's best balladeer, continuing the trend that began with "Creep" on the fuzzed-out, tortured torch songs "Big Empty" and "Still Remains," a pretty fucked-up love song on which Weiland sings, "Take a bath—I'll drink the water that you leave." That's a level of devotion that might only be topped by "I wish I could eat your cancer." These guys had issues—no wonder everybody was on Prozac.

After *Purple*, STP never really had a great album (though their *Purple* follow-up, *Tiny Music . . . Songs from the Vatican Gift Shop*, was largely excellent), and they ended up indulging in their psychedelic tendencies and devolving into a very boring version of the Doors, only to break up very passively when Weiland joined the Guns N' Roses castoffs to form Velvet Revolver, which might be the most logical career choice in the history of man. *Purple* remains Stone Temple Pilots' masterpiece, and though they seemed like pure evil at the time, STP was a pretty excellent rock band that wrote some of the most killer tunes of the era. If anything, this album will always be underrated because the band was so easy to hate. It'll never be all that important, but it will still rock.

TEMPLE OF THE DOG, *Temple of the Dog* (A&M, 1991): Considering its members were the best parts of Pearl Jam and Soundgarden, Temple of the Dog should be the best band of the grunge era and the greatest supergroup of all time. Of course they only got together for one album, and that album didn't gain recognition until well after Pearl Jam broke out, so its cultural relevance is somewhat suspect. But *Temple of the Dog* remains a fascinating landmark that would make this list based on personnel alone. Created as a tribute to deceased Mother Love Bone front man Andrew Wood, *Temple of the Dog* acts as a sort of eulogy for the group's fallen friend. There's a sort of "Irish wake" quality to the record, which is mostly midtempo tunes played with surprising energy. Despite the fact that Chris Cornell handles most of the vocal duties, the album bears a much greater resemblance to Pearl Jam's classic rock leanings than to Soundgarden's arena metal, and it has a looseness that makes it clear it was written and recorded pretty much on the fly. Because of that looseness, there's probably only enough quality stuff here to make up a pretty great EP and nothing more, and some of the songs are bloated and meandering. However, the chemistry between the band members cannot be denied, making *Temple of the Dog* one of the best illustrations of the true sense of community and brotherhood that many of the grunge-era musicians had—especially those actually living in Seattle.

The best-known songs from *Temple of the Dog* are the two that made it onto rock radio: "Say Hello 2 Heaven," an epic about the afterlife, and "Hunger Strike," a pretty rocking song that features an amazing back-and-forth vocal between Vedder and Cornell and a music video that had Jeff Ament playing in a tree in one of the silliest images of the nineties. The album also acts as a pretty excellent tribute to Wood, as it shares so much sonic quality (and actual band members) with Mother Love Bone that it sort of seems like the final, unreleased MLB album. Wood would have been proud.

MATTHEW SWEET, *100% Fun* (Zoo, 1995): Every generation needs their own Alex Chilton: a guy who doesn't really belong to any one genre but manages to make very pretty records playing in just about everybody's backyard, and who does all this in a fairly controlling, vaguely maladjusted fashion. Elvis Costello kind of became the Chilton of the eighties, and the seventies had the real Chilton. Matthew Sweet, for better or for worse, acted as the nineties Chilton (the twenty-first century Chilton would probably be Jack White or DJ Danger Mouse). Sweet's early albums were the same kind of stomping, anthemic power pop that Chilton perfected in Big Star twenty years prior, and the sound was tweaked and made just dirty enough where Sweet was associated with the grunge guys. "Girlfriend," from his 1991 album of the same name, was a huge modern rock hit and was about the most genuine love song of the era. Sweet was devoted to traditional, Beatlesy pop-rock songcraft, but he was more than happy to turn it on its ear once in a while. *100% Fun* represents his most balanced and hardest-rocking work. While "Girlfriend" is still his most important and best-known track, *100% Fun* featured some great songs that showed off guitarist Richard Lloyd's (of Television fame) twisting, spiraling guitar style. The awesomely fuzzed-out Creep Rocker "Sick of Myself" was a hit on modern rock radio and features some tight guitar noodling, something that was always considered off-limits in grunge circles. Other highlights include the Neil Young–channeling "Super Baby," the shimmering "We're the Same," and the intense, stuttering wash of "Lost My Mind."

Sweet's croon isn't very dynamic, but it does the job, and lyrically he wavers between being a hopeless romantic, a manipulative creep, and a self-loathing slacker, somehow combining an emo guy, Weiland, and Beck into one incredible front-man package. He never made another great album after this one, as he jettisoned Lloyd and ended up playing almost every instrument on the 1997 follow-up, *Blue Sky on Mars*. Subsequent Sweet material has veered into layered California pop—perhaps he's trying to become more Brian Wilson and less Alex Chilton (neither seems like a great role model). But Sweet's work on *100% Fun* has stood up, which says a lot for his songcraft and his ability to write melodies. Perhaps the best aspect of *100% Fun* is its title: It's one instance of jubilation from the grunge era that doesn't seem at all ironic, so at the absolute worst, Sweet will be remembered as the guy who smiled and said, "I love you," amid all the shrugging and brooding.

VERUCA SALT, *American Thighs* (Minty Fresh/DGC, 1994): **Named** after the infamous "I Want It Now" character from *Willy Wonka and the Chocolate Factory*, Veruca Salt came out of Chicago and fashioned themselves as a dirty, scratchy midperiod alternative force that picked up right around where the Breeders had left off. Veruca Salt also had a serious Beatles fixation: Co–front women Louise Post and Nina Gordon operated in a Lennon/McCartney model, with the sweeter, infectious pop songs of Gordon mixing with Post's more jagged, outside-the-box take. *American Thighs* also opens with a song called "Get Back," and their sophomore album,

Eight Arms to Hold You (itself a Beatles reference), even contains a wacky White Album in-joke where they echo the "walrus was Paul" line from "Glass Onion." Of course, *American Thighs* doesn't have the same sort of staying power as a Beatles record, but it does rock pretty hard. The album has a raw, open-wound quality that makes it sound like it was produced by Steve Albini. The guitars sound claustrophobic, the bass is floaty and metallic, and the drums are shallow but imposing. On top of it all are the harmonies of Post and Gordon, whose gorgeous vocal lines often mask the siren wails of the songs beneath them. There isn't a whole lot of wiggle room with these songs—Veruca Salt figured out what their sound was and basically didn't waver from it for the length of their existence. But there are some subtle variations among the tracks, from the Zeppelinesque "All Hail Me" to the grinding push-pull of "Spiderman '79."

People often forget that grunge was pretty much a boys club; outside of Hole, Veruca Salt was basically the only female-led band that played this type of music and actually got a bit of recognition for it—"Seether" was a huge hit, and *American Thighs* sold gold. It probably helped that "Seether" was as ubiquitous as it was and that both Post and Gordon were superfoxy, but the hard-charging, metallic sexuality of *American Thighs* stuck to the ribs of post-Cobain rock and roll just fine.

RAGE AGAINST THE MACHINE, *Rage Against the Machine* (Epic, 1992): Musically, aesthetically, and philosophically, Rage Against the Machine has never been like *anybody*. Plenty of people had experimented with adding the chocolate of rap music to the peanut butter of hard rock, but Rage was the first band that made it sound good, and they also made it sound *important*, and that had little to do with front man Zack de la Rocha's political leanings. Even a decade and a half later, Rage's self-titled debut still sounds as raw, as desperate, and as heavy as ever. In truth, they don't belong anywhere on this list—outside of the fact that Rage was booked on Lollapalooza, the band had pretty much no relationship to the alt-rock world. They were played on modern rock radio, but this album was originally absorbed as a metal album (and rightfully so). The three non–de la Rocha members of Rage later joined forces with Chris Cornell to form Audioslave, but that band sounds like the most talented seventies cover band in history—it seems like they should be releasing a very faithful version of "Don't Fear the Reaper" at any time (perhaps drummer Brad Wilk is perfecting his cowbell). Wilk was friends with Eddie Vedder—that's about the best anybody can do for a grunge link.

In a continuing theme, it's more important that Rage Against the Machine became big *when* they did rather than *how* they did. Had grunge never happened, Rage would have been treated like a very esoteric metal band (like Anthrax, who had also experimented with hip-hop) rather than cultural icons. After all, rap-rock didn't properly break until years later when Fred Durst showed up to break stuff. But because of the grunge-era openness, Rage Against the Machine was elevated to pop-star level. In any other time, they might have been ghettoized for being difficult to place in a bin at the record store, but during the early nineties, they stood out as another band that was thinking outside the box. They couldn't have come at a better time, as their combination of socially aware altruism and fiery metal angst was fully understood in the musical climate of 1992. Rage was just like Pearl Jam, except taken to the *n*th degree—they were more concerned with worldly affairs than family drama, and they did it with a far more aggressive sound.

De la Rocha screaming, "Fuck you, I won't do what you tell me," will forever represent all the grunge kids who fought with their parents or had a party that was broken up by the cops. Of course,

"Killing in the Name" was about police officers who were also members of the KKK, but that disconnect between their intentions and their audience was always a cornerstone in Rage Against the Machine's charm.

Rage was known first for de la Rocha's wailing about Zapatistas and second for guitarist Tom Morello's six-string theatrics, but Rage's secret weapon was always their rhythm section, who could play plodding metal, jumpy funk, and soaring anthemic rock with equal aplomb and make it all sound logical and badass. Rage flamed out at the turn of the millennium after two more spectacular studio albums. Most of the band became Audioslave, and de la Rocha went into an Axl Rose–ish state of seclusion, supposedly working on a high-profile album with multiple producers that may never get released (again, just like Axl). Though they'll likely be blamed for setting the precedent that allowed for the rise of Limp Bizkit and countless other rap-metal bands that seized airwaves around the turn of the millennium, few bands made the sort of impact that Rage did across so many boundaries and with such little musical output–ten years, three proper studio albums, and only thirty-some songs.

SCREAMING TREES, *Dust* (Epic, 1996): Led by the bluesy, gravelly voice of front man and chief songwriter Mark Lanegan, Screaming Trees was a band from Seattle that had more or less found their sound by the time the rest of the universe started noticing the Pacific Northwest, and though they had a couple of big singles (most notably "Nearly Lost You," from their 1992 album, *Sweet Oblivion*), they were never able to break out the way that their peers did. Screaming Trees' vision was unwavering, but they improved slightly in both sound and songcraft, which is why *Dust*, their final studio album, is their greatest achievement.

Screaming Trees was probably the most psychedelic of any of

the Seattle bands. While groups like Stone Temple Pilots trafficked in theatrical, Doorsian psych sounds, Screaming Trees had more of a garage psych sound, dragging in low-fi spindles of Eastern influences and trippy backyard keyboard effects that meshed nicely with Lanegan's haunting, otherworldly voice. *Dust* is an impressive culmination of a career's worth of development. "Traveler" is an excellent example: Rugged acoustic guitars swirl around distorted strings and flute noises while Lanegan moans about getting "halfway there." Lanegan also has a penchant for dusty biblical imagery—he mentions the Lord making him stay in "All I Know" and cries with Mary during "Dying Days." When these are combined with the epic quality of the music, *Dust* creates an incredible mood of things being over, as though it's being played live at the end-times. It's as though the band knew this would be their last album together—or as though they knew that the scene they were a part of was slowly turning to dust.

MUDHONEY, *Every Good Boy Deserves Fudge* (Sub Pop, 1991): Of all the post–Green River grunge bands, Mudhoney was absolutely the purest. Front man/songwriter/mad scientist Mark Arm was responsible for coining the term "grunge," and later constructing the sort of sound that grunge would represent. Arm came close to his vision of sonic purity with Green River, but the guys who ended up forming Pearl Jam dragged the band too far in the arena-metal direction. Mudhoney represents Arm's idealized rock band: equal parts punk, noise, metal, garage, and a whole lot of wailing and sweat.

Though it doesn't contain "Touch Me I'm Sick," the one song Mudhoney is best known for, which was released as a single on Sub Pop in 1988 and was later folded into the rerelease of their *Superfuzz Bigmuff* EP, *Every Good Boy Deserves Fudge* represents Mudhoney's best-sounding and most consistent album. Ironically, it's probably also their least "grunge"-sounding album, as the whole thing feels slightly faster and tighter than their other recordings and thus gives them a slightly more polished sound. But that's a sliding scale, as this record still sounds wild, raw, and sort of filthy. Opening blast "Generation Genocide" acts as a wonderful warm-up for "Let It Slide," a speedy garage freak-out that deftly show-cases Arm's nasal, snotty delivery. Elsewhere on the album, the band sounds as though they've been listening to a lot of Thirteenth Floor Elevators records, as an organ and a harmonica both creep into the mix, and both have the tossed-off quality that says, "Hey! We found this lying around the studio!" That's not to say the Mud-honey band members were lazy or not accomplished musicians, but they have the energy of a pack of punk-drunk teenagers—amazing considering Arm was already pushing thirty by the time *Every Good Boy Deserves Fudge* came out.

Mudhoney later signed a major-label deal with Reprise Records and their sound devolved back into the *Superfuzz Bigmuff* era "clas-sic grunge." Though they never sold a ton of records and usually got their greatest exposure as an opening act for their friends in Pearl Jam and Soundgarden, Arm's influence still ran deep, as it seemed like everybody in Seattle was constantly seeking his ap-proval. Eddie Vedder was constantly talking in the press about how much more famous Mudhoney should be, but Arm's band acted as a great equalizer among modern rock fans in that era, be-cause if you were down with Mudhoney, it meant you were a more serious rock fan than other people. When looked at that way, Mudhoney just becomes a less successful version of Tool, and there are certainly worse fates (like being a less successful version of Interpol, for example).

LEMONHEADS, *It's a Shame About Ray* (Atlantic, 1992): **No matter how weird your 1992 was, there's no way it could have possibly** been more odd than Evan Dando's. The Lemonheads front man went from relative obscurity writing vaguely punkish doe-eyed love songs in Boston to being named one of *People*'s sexiest men alive, all on the strength of a twenty-five-year-old song. Suddenly that summer when you ate nothing but cheese Danishes while trying to figure out how e-mail worked must seem a little tame.

Dando's band first gained major exposure with a cover of Simon and Garfunkel's "Mrs. Robinson," which was recorded in association with the anniversary video release of *The Graduate*. Initial pressings of *It's a Shame About Ray* did not include the track, but when it started getting radio play and people started noticing Dando, it was tacked on as a bonus track (it's now hard to find a version that doesn't contain it). Breaking into the mainstream with a cover is usually a recipe for disaster (just ask the guys in Alien Ant Farm or Orgy), but luckily the cover was associated with Dando's most fluid, heartfelt, powerful album. The title track is the sort of dreamy, strum-heavy dirge that twentysomethings used so they wouldn't freak out while getting high, and it was delivered with Dando's tossed-off "I'm just a bummed-out guy with a guitar" feel. He represented slacker nation to a T. There's no doubt that had he used his songwriting skills with any sort of commitment, he could have been the Goo Goo Dolls.

Still, even with his why-bother demeanor, Dando became an accidental icon, something that only could have happened in the grunge era. While he never scored a hit as big as "Mrs. Robinson" ("If I Could Talk I'd Tell You," from 1996's *Car Button Cloth*, was probably the next closest), Dando did make a permanent mark on the generation's music, and his rise to almost ubiquity is a perfect encapsulation of how incredibly open-minded the populace was at the turn of the nineties. Dando didn't do much to capitalize on his fame—he let his songs speak for him, and with angsty suburban gems such as "Confetti" and "My Drug Buddy," it's no wonder that people are still attached to the very idea of the guy in the sense that his subsequent solo albums have been mostly forgettable, but there is still a buzz around every single one of their releases—more proof that both fans and critics have a hard time letting go.

FOO FIGHTERS, *Foo Fighters* (Roswell/Capitol, 1995): **People have** never really known how to absorb Dave Grohl. When he sat behind the drum kit in Nirvana, he was just a manic explosion of hair and limbs that never seemed to talk. Once that band went kaput, he stepped in front of a microphone and fronted his own band, Foo Fighters. Through more than ten years and several million albums, people have always given Grohl not nearly enough credit (many of his best songs, such as "Everlong" and "Learn to Fly," have been written off as "soft") or entirely too much credit (Grohl was looked upon to "save" rock and roll on several albums, never really fulfilling that potential). The only time he ever got the correct, rational amount of props was when he sat in on drums for Queens of the Stone Age's *Songs for the Deaf*, which was a wonderfully dynamic record that Grohl really left his mark on.

In truth, Grohl's career is pretty remarkable, and for a guy whose iconic band had just fallen apart, the self-titled debut from his new group, Foo Fighters, is nothing short of miraculous. Most of the songs contained on *Foo Fighters* were written while Grohl was still in Nirvana, so many of them have an *In Utero*-ish feel to them (though the production on *Foo Fighters* is *way* cleaner than Steve Albini would have wanted it). This is especially evident on primal screams such as "Watershed" and "Weenie Beenie," but the fuzz on tracks such as "Exhausted" and "X-Static" has Kurt's fingerprints on it as well. That's not to say Grohl was just making a lesser Nirvana album, as songs such as "Big Me" (which birthed the legendary Mentos-spoofing video that made Grohl an MTV staple) and "For All the Cows" have a breeziness about them that keeps the overall tone way less angsty. Grohl wasn't a total goofball, but he did realize the dangers in taking himself too seriously.

Because Grohl plays every instrument on every song (save for some guitar noodling on "X-Static" care of the Afghan Whigs' Greg Dulli), *Foo Fighters* is best absorbed as a solo album. Lyrically and sonically it works better that way, as this album has a certain claustrophobic feeling that never really showed up on subsequent Foos releases. When Grohl did put his band together, he chose former Germs guitarist and sometimes Nirvana touring axman Pat Smear, along with the rhythm section from Seattle emo quartet Sunny Day Real Estate, and though that lineup didn't last long, it was the ideal group of musicians to carry out Grohl's vision, which was a little bit gutter punk, a little bit glam, and a whole lot of heart-on-sleeve longing. Just about any single Foo Fighters has put out is better than any of the songs on this debut, but *Foo Fighters* acted as an amazing transition album between what we knew of grunge and what it would become. After all, if one of the guys *in* Nirvana didn't want to sound like Nirvana, what chance did anybody else have?

DEEP SIX (C/Z Records, 1986): There are two compilations that helped to plant the seeds of the grunge sound and began creating the lines that linked otherwise disparate noise bands. The more notable of the two is *Sub Pop 100*, the first compilation release from the then-brand-new Sub Pop Records. It featured at least one legendary band (Sonic Youth), a smattering of grunge forefathers (U-Men, the Wipers), and a couple of bands that would later appear way, way out of context (Skinny Puppy, Shonen Knife). It's a record that gets better with age, considering the quality of the tracks and the incredibly low production values at the time, but it better illustrated what Sub Pop would later become (and what it currently is)—a catchall indie label whose philosophy is to have no philosophy.

But *Deep Six* came first, beating *Sub Pop 100* by a handful of months. More important, it had a much more cohesive structure and a relatively singular approach to what sorts of bands were on it. The "Six" in question were Green River, Malfunkshun, the Melvins, Skin Yard, Soundgarden, and the U-Men. Each of those bands was absolutely seminal and influential to the grunge sound.

It gets by on history alone, but the quality of the tracks on the compilation has actually stood the test of time. Green River was a brand-new band, yet "10,000 Things" already shows them knee-deep in their push-pull between noisy metal screeching and arena-rock boogie. "Stars-N-You" is by far the best song Malfunkshun ever put out (which is not saying all that much, but it remains true). The two songs by Skin Yard, "Throb" and "The Birds," are awesome slices of trippy, sludgy psychedelic mumbo jumbo. It's a sound that Skin Yard would quickly grow out of (the band later rerecorded both songs, and the new versions have almost no relationship to these original tries—though they certainly *rock* a little more), but it does provide a good jumping-off point for the production style of Skin Yard guitarist and "Godfather of Grunge" Jack Endino, the producer who would later produce breakout work by Soundgarden, Nirvana, Mudhoney, and most everybody else living in Seattle with a guitar between 1988 and 1995.

Of course, the charms of this document (which is quite hard to find nowadays) are the same as the detriments: The production values are cartoonishly low, and the record revolves around four middle-of-the-road Melvins songs, which are a bit of an acquired taste. But the history remains, and it's worth noting for the Soundgarden songs alone, as they are *unbelievably* heavy.

BUSH, *Sixteen Stone* (Trauma/Interscope, 1994): Before the music media got ahold of him, Gavin Rossdale was just a slightly pretentious art student from suburban England. By the time everybody had taken a shot at him, he might as well have been one of the four horsemen of the Apocalypse (probably famine, considering his chiseled body). In reality, while Gavin's band Bush didn't totally undo everything Kurt, Eddie, and the rest of the Seattleites had built, it certainly represented the beginning of the end. After all, Bush did take a sound that was pure and visceral and managed to break it out into its simplest form. If four arty Englishmen can do it, who's to stop *anybody* from picking apart the scraps?

Actually, when viewed as a sociological experiment or an art project, *Sixteen Stone* might actually be one of the finest accomplishments in Western history. Its grunge distilled to its purest form, to a point where it almost ceases to exist as a whole. The pieces are so clearly separated out and then combined together into songs that the entire record is almost wholly incoherent. That does not sound like a compliment, but it is. The twelve songs on *Sixteen Stone* sound *exactly* like what grunge is supposed to sound like, while the whole point of grunge was that it didn't really sound like *anything*, including itself. Just consider how many different bands and styles of music have been shoved under the "grunge" header in this discography alone, and you realize that grunge is probably the most ill-defined genre of music in history. But one guy actually went ahead and established a definition, and that guy's name is Gavin Rossdale. By this measure, *Sixteen Stone* is the only truly perfect grunge album, and that's its greatest achievement but also its greatest flaw—its a stunning feat of execution of a genre that was all about imperfection.

Though many people won't admit it, the songs on *Sixteen Stone* are pretty awesome, especially the singles "Everything Zen," "Little Things," and "Comedown," which stole the bass line from Bon Jovi's "Livin' on a Prayer." Actually, the Bon Jovi metaphor works fairly well: Bush was always desperate for attention and critical recognition but settled for having the more popular songs and selling more records. Like Jon Bon Jovi, Gavin Rossdale always seemed too pretty to be singing about the things he sang about (although his lyrics were always fairly incoherent, so who really knows *what* he was singing about). Gavin never wrote a batch of songs better than these, and the rest of Bush's albums ended up floating from genre to genre (their sophomore release was a Steve Albini–produced arena noise album called *Razorblade Suitcase*, which was followed by a sort of futuristic-sounding robot rock record called *The Science of Things*). *Sixteen Stone* represented Rossdale's *Slippery When Wet*. If only he had come ten years earlier and wore more denim—he could have been a star!

MOTHER LOVE BONE, *Apple* (Polydor, 1990): The universe works in very odd ways, and rock and roll is as subject to its random machinations as anything. Mother Love Bone was designed to be a Great (capital *G*) rock band. They had a hard-rocking sound. They had a will to succeed. They had a unique, dynamic front man. They had epic, killer songs. Yet the album that was supposed to be their coming-out party ended up acting as their funeral march, as front man Andrew Wood died before *Apple* could hit store shelves. Mother Love Bone's music never really made an impact until after Pearl Jam broke (and really not until people heard Temple of the Dog). Whether or not Mother Love Bone would have had any sort of breakthrough is up for debate, but there is no denying this record. Like any good album that aspires to be the perfect arena record, *Apple* is all about the ballads. Certainly the Aerosmith-channeling boogie rock of "Stardog Champion" and "This Is Shangrila" is both infectious and inventive, but *Apple*'s strengths lie in the epic scope of "Crown of Thorns." A true lighter burner, it begins quietly and slowly builds into a deafening crescendo as Wood wails like a preacher on fire—think of it as a nineties' "Dream On." It's that good.

Apple is a remarkable little artifact because it was clearly written and produced to be played on the radio, which cast it in an entirely different league from any of its contemporaries (such as Nirvana's *Bleach* or Soundgarden's *Ultramega OK*). When taken in the context of other great grunge albums, *Apple* sounds almost entirely out of context, as the only thing "indie" about it is the production quality. At the same time, *Apple* did express all of the possibilities that Pearl Jam would later transform into greatness—consider it a warm-up for *Ten*. Even as a rehearsal, it's still impressive.

PEARL JAM, *Vitalogy* (Epic, 1994): Released toward the end of 1994, *Vitalogy* is not only one of the best albums of the grunge era but also one of the most interesting albums of the twentieth century. Whether it was intentional or not, Pearl Jam managed to distill everything that was remarkable about them *and* everything that was making them frustrating all into one spectacular package. The band released *Vitalogy* on vinyl a few weeks before it was released on CD, ostensibly to reward fans who were purists and still listened to their turntables. Unfortunately, the gambit didn't pay off, as all it did was flood the market with scratchy, popping bootleg versions of the album before anybody could buy their clean CD copy. It was another prime example of Pearl Jam really going out with the best of intentions and shooting themselves in the foot (see also: Ticketmaster).

But all stunts aside, *Vitalogy* represents Pearl Jam at their rawest and most unhinged, which is a strange thing to say considering the sheer number of ballads present. That's okay, because even the ballads have an exposed-nerve quality, as though Pearl Jam managed to find their most basic essence, but every minute it's exposed is painful. Midtempo rockers "Last Exit" and "Not for You" see Eddie Vedder at his angriest and most loathsome. He lashes out at people who would take what's his, and he's not interested in compromise. It often seems like *Vitalogy* represents what Pearl Jam *is actually like*, as if they somehow figured out how to be totally honest as people for exactly one album. They didn't sound this upfront before and haven't since.

Of course, all that transparency does lead to goofy experiments such as Vedder's accordion solo, "Bugs," and the eerie-but-listless collage "Heyfoxymophandlemomma, That's Me." Credit is due, though, as Pearl Jam felt so emboldened that they let all their whims hang out, which was a rarity in the hyper-self-aware nineties.

But the big story on *Vitalogy* is the slow jams, which float up and weave in and out and fade away and flash forward in the most gorgeous, raw ways possible. "Better Man" describes the profound sense of loss that accompanies giving up on aspirations and settling for comfort. "Immortality" muses on death with the help of some awesomely sad slide guitars, and "Nothingman" just about sums up the length of the grunge era and Pearl Jam's entire career in about five minutes. "Caught a bolt of lightning," sings Vedder. "Curse the day he let it go." Since this was the first Pearl Jam album to hit the street after the death of Cobain, Eddie Vedder should have rightfully taken his place as the spokesman for a generation's rock fans, but he (gracefully) bowed out of the position, mostly by being distracted by his fight with Ticketmaster (there was nothing especially "rocking" about warring with a gigantic corporation, and kids actually felt slightly betrayed that Pearl Jam concentrated more on fighting their regulations than on actual *touring*). Since the release of *Vitalogy* (generally agreed among Pearl Jam fans to be their finest hour), Pearl Jam has flirted with excellence but mostly has come up short one way or another. *Vitalogy* tells a loose story about death and loss and sacrifice, yet it is by far the most energetic and "up" of all the Pearl Jam albums. While their latter-day experiments tend to err on the side of garagey rocking, their talent still lies in crafting heartbreaking songs of sadness and loss. "He who forgets," sings Eddie in "Nothingman," "will be destined to remember." Pearl Jam never figured out how to be as good as *Vitalogy*, so perhaps they will one day come around back to it.

NIRVANA, *Unplugged in New York* (DGC, 1994): Issued a mere eight months after Cobain's suicide, *Unplugged in New York* initially seemed like an odd forum for Nirvana to fully participate in, but over time it's shown that it was a perfect marriage of sound and substance. *Spin magazine* once projected that "folktronica" would be the next big thing, and it's hard to imagine that this live recording didn't have a huge effect on that particular prediction. It's hard to blame them—Cobain was a tastemaker, and he had decided that he was getting into solo acoustic songs, Leadbelly covers, and the farm punk of his friends in the Meat Puppets. The world never got the chance to see what Kurt would do next (at least musically), so nobody ever has to worry about Kurt's Pete Seeger tribute album. But the passion with which Kurt attacked the songs on *Unplugged in New York* made it seem like the world was dealing with a whole new Kurt, a Kurt who could joke and cope. A Kurt with a voracious appetite for melody and simplicity. It's no wonder this guy recorded with Steve Albini.

Actually, it's strange to talk about this album as a Nirvana project, considering how many covers are included in the performance. Kurt's own songs sound enlightened, as though he rescued them from exile and needed to nurse them back to health. This is especially true on *In Utero* tracks such as "Dumb" and "Pennyroyal Tea." But the album is truly notable for the songs Cobain didn't write. The trifecta of Meat Puppets tunes are all excellent and certainly *feel* like Nirvana songs (especially "Plateau"), and the Leadbelly cover (a version of "In the Pines" titled "Where Did You Sleep Last Night?") is an amazing four minutes of music. It ended up being Cobain's last recorded song, but it made absolute sense in more ways than one. The obtuse lyrics, the esoteric voice, the careerist tendencies, the general sense of malcontentment—Cobain was evolving into a next-generation Bob Dylan right before the alt-rock audience's eyes, except Kurt went electric first, then tried acoustic.

Much like Mother Love Bone's *Apple, Unplugged in New York* acted as both an exciting new chapter and an ad hoc tribute to a fallen icon. It mostly displays Cobain's skills as a songwriter and arranger, but it also illustrates how varied the influences were on grunge, a genre that was the bastard son of a thousand subcultures.

HOLE, *Live Through This* (DGC, 1994): All of Courtney Love's career will forever be wrapped up in that of her late husband, Kurt Cobain, but even if she released a Nirvana covers album, nothing will ever live in the shadow of Kurt quite like *Live Through This*. This album's very existence had some people convinced that Love had Cobain murdered, as its tone and release date seemed a little too convenient at the time. Even the title suggests that the widow Love is daring anybody else to survive what she was in the process of surviving. Mention *Live Through This*, and most people will think immediately about the Cobain connection.

The other accusation that Courtney had to fend off was that she wasn't responsible for the songs on the album and that her husband had written them for her. Again, the circumstantial evidence is pretty profound, as Love's band Hole went from sounding like an amorphous noise rock outfit on their debut album, *Pretty on the Inside*, to sounding exactly like the arena-ready screamers that were clogging the airwaves circa 1994. Whether it was Cobain's influence or she was just capitalizing on a sonic trend, there was something about *Live Though This* that seemed disingenuous, and it's unlikely that the truth will ever fully come out.

None of that matters, however. The more time passes, the less important the details of this album become. In the end, it's about the songs, and even if Courtney didn't write them, they still sound absolutely amazing. Hole's command of the quiet verse/loud chorus dynamic was unmatched by anybody, including Nirvana. Album opener "Violet" is a prime example: It begins with a jagged muted guitar strum and some simple woodblocks, then explodes into a fireball of a guitar riff as Love screams, "Go on take everything!" over and over again. It's a perfect storm of a song and one of the best radio tunes from that era.

Elsewhere, the band tears through raw, unforgiving bludgeon jobs such as "Asking for It" and "Softer, Softest" with reckless abandon. There is very little letting up on *Live Through This*–"Doll Parts" is probably the closest thing Hole gets to playing a "ballad"–but the unbridled rage is quite a thing to behold. Some people complain that the album sounds too slick, but it's the sort of slick that worked for Nirvana–when you don't have to worry about making something sound messy and chaotic, you can just allow it to be messy and chaotic.

Live Through This is a great record taken out of context; given its history, it morphs into an Important (capital *I*) album. Time will tell whether or not it was remembered for the right reasons, but like it or not, Hole dragged the riot grrrl movement into the spotlight and gave a mainstream voice to angry girls everywhere (if nothing else, Love inspired Alanis Morissette, though Alanis was equally inspired by Dave Coulier). Though Kurt was always talking about female empowerment and the music certainly seemed less sexist than hair metal was, grunge was still mostly a boys club. For one album, Courtney Love had bigger balls than anybody, and she wasn't afraid to show them off.

SOUNDGARDEN, *Superunknown* (A&M, 1994): Though it's the most traditional and most esoteric-sounding Soundgarden album, *Superunknown* is the album that made Chris Cornell and company into superstars, and perhaps at no time in history was a band's sound ever so *functional.* In 1994, Soundgarden was the total package: They looked like heshers, they played like giants, and they wrote songs that sounded like well-groomed mastodons plowing through the countryside.

Superunknown is undoubtedly the least metal-sounding album Soundgarden ever produced, but they still wear their Sabbath on their sleeves, as evidenced by the opening riff to just about every track here (but most notably on "Black Hole Sun," which sounds like what the Beatles would sound like if they were turned up superloud and then forced to drink nothing but absinthe for eight straight days). But unlike *Badmotorfinger*, Soundgarden isn't afraid to play around with grunge's goofy sense of humor, hence tracks such as "Spoonman" and "My Wave." Soundgarden never sounded like they listened to a punk album, but they certainly sped the pace up and introduced a new speed to co-opt their heavy plod on tracks such as the feisty "Kickstand." And of course there was the ever-present darkness of "Fell on Black Days" and "The Day I Tried to Live," both of which are incredibly depressing sorta-suicide ballads that still manage to sound like arena anthems. Eat your heart out, Rob Halford.

If anyone ever asks for a really good example of how unbelievably popular grunge was circa 1994, lay this story on them: That year, when this album came out, the song "Spoonman" became a pretty big hit. "Spoonman," which is a song about a guy playing spoons that was written as a joke, featured a video that was just a guy playing spoons, and *contained a goddamn spoons solo*, was a pretty big hit (said video was in *very* heavy rotation on MTV, back when that actually meant something). "Spoonman" is probably the most ridiculous song to ever reach the top of MTV's video chart. Grunge was so huge that the populace not only allowed for that to happen but encouraged it to come into existence. It's likely looked upon as a big joke now, but the fact remains that for at least a while "Spoonman" was pretty ubiquitous, marking grunge as the world's most powerful delivery system for just about anything.

SMASHING PUMPKINS, *Siamese Dream* (Virgin, 1993): One of pop music's all-time great "The Chicken or the Egg" debates is whether Billy Corgan had a persecution complex because nobody liked him or nobody liked him because he had a persecution complex. Corgan was one of the most prolific and successful songwriters of the nineties and commanded legions of adoring fans, but it always seemed like everybody just *hated* the guy. From journalists to other musicians and even (or especially) bandmates, Corgan was clearly a hard gentleman to know. He's mellowed since his Smashing Pumpkins heyday, but that doesn't take away his history of being difficult.

One could imagine that one of the reasons people might have turned on Corgan was the monstrous success of *Siamese Dream*, the second album from Smashing Pumpkins. It's a remarkable record because it sounds like an alt-rock record (the guitars are fuzzy and detuned; Corgan's lyrics are generally melancholy) but also separates itself from the pack (the production, by *Gish* and *Nevermind* knob twiddler Butch Vig, sounds absolutely massive, and there are a lot of nonironic seventies rock flourishes such as guitar and drum solos). *Siamese Dream* wants nothing to do with being cool, as Smashing Pumpkins had already done that on *Gish.* Rather, *Siamese Dream* wanted to sound epic, like the greatest album of all time.

It falls short of that goal (it's not even the greatest album on this list), but it certainly makes a hell of an effort and clears a lot of hurdles along the way. The album opens with "Cherub Rock," a song that perfectly defines the Pumpkins' style and how *Siamese Dream* was to be defined: big-sounding, rolling drums, alternately humming and screaming guitars, and, most important Billy Corgan, he of nasal vocal qualities and interesting phrasing. It sounds like an outtake from a Boston album, but the chorus is pure 1993—over a hook so expansive you could fly a 747 through it, Corgan wails, "Let me out!" With that combination of a pedigree, it's no wonder "Cherub Rock" became a modern rock radio staple and will likely make a very smooth transition into "classic rock."

Another amazing thing about *Siamese Dream* was the fact that it was really, truly an *album.* Mainstream rock records that were actually constructed as long players and not just a string of singles were common in the early nineties; before that, the metal albums of the eighties were mostly anthems surrounded by throwaways (with a handful of major exceptions, obviously). Grunge rockers took most of their cues from seventies rockers, so they knew the value of a CD that plays like an LP—a full, focused, hour-plus experience that rewarded faithful listeners with subtleties and quirks. *Siamese Dream* almost plays like a concept album, or is at least paced like one, as "Cherub Rock" is followed by the buzzsaw-esque rocker "Quiet," then the band launches into three straight epic anthems ("Today," "Hummer," and "Rocket") before settling into a theatrical ballad ("Disarm") to end act 1. The story arc of *Siamese*

Dream basically boils down to "Billy Corgan is complicated," but *Siamese Dream* is one of the few long players from the grunge era that still sounds reasonable as a full-length today.

Of course, Corgan took that concept to the extreme with his next record, the double-disc *Mellon Collie and the Infinite Sadness* that *is* actually a concept album (its story arc is "Billy Corgan is *really* complicated"), but the Pumpkins will be remembered for *Siamese Dream*, and rightfully so. Years from now, it will probably sound slightly out of place among its contemporaries (compared to *In Utero* or *Superunknown* or *Dirt*, it sounds kind of wussy or at least overtly commercial), but in reality Corgan did the only thing that was truly "alternative" in 1993: He wrote an album in an attempt to be a rock star. While everybody else was hiding, Corgan said, "Look at me"—no wonder everybody turned on this dude.

SINGLES original soundtrack (Epic Soundtrax, 1992): It's sort of unfair to have compilations on this list (and so high up to boot), but this is a stunning collection that perfectly personifies the rock-and-roll landscape circa 1992. *Singles* covers just about all the bases, and if there was a Nirvana song on this album, it would probably catapult itself to number one. As it stands, it's still pretty impressive.

Cameron Crowe's movies are essentially mix tapes that happen to end up on film, and considering how close Crowe was with the bands involved (several of them appear in the film, most notably three members of Pearl Jam as the non–Matt Dillon members of Citizen Dick), it's no wonder this record sounds so good. But just as *Singles* accidentally defined a generation, the sound track to the movie ended up defining a great deal of grunge's musical aesthetic by showing audiences exactly what (and who) was involved. Ironically, the most vital contributions to *Singles* came from Paul

Westerberg, whose "Dyslexic Heart" and "Waiting for Somebody" were the first songs he released as a solo artist after the breakup of the Replacements, a band considered to be an essential influence on the grunge sound (Kurt Cobain often threw Westerberg props in interviews). Westerberg's contributions showed listeners where some of this grunge stuff was coming from, so it made the transition to a song such as Pearl Jam's "State of Love and Trust" (probably the second or third best song in the band's catalog and a dead ringer for a sped-up version of a midperiod Replacements track) seem smooth and logical. The album also featured songs by Mother Love Bone and the Lovemongers (who were really just an acoustic version of Heart), bands that not only contributed kick-ass tunes (Lovemongers even covered Zeppelin!) but also gave grunge a context. It was a disorienting and confusing one, but it was a context nonetheless.

Alice in Chains probably owes Cameron Crowe their entire success. While *Facelift* was getting attention, it was the appearance of "Would?" on this sound track that really put them on the map. It also contains the best Mudhoney song ever written in "Overblown" and first showed the world both sides of Soundgarden, on the heavy-as-Thor's-hammer "Birth Ritual" and on Chris Cornell's acoustic "Seasons." It even invites Billy Corgan to the party, as Smashing Pumpkins' dirgey "Drown" closes out the record—it can even be argued that the inclusion on *Singles* allowed Corgan to be embraced by the greater alt-rock community, as Smashing Pumpkins was one of the first non-Seattle bands to really capitalize off of the scene *and* be met with a shred of critical respect.

So *Singles* is essentially a perfect storm of an album: It has incredible songs by a group of artists who were relevant but whose importance was increased a hundredfold by their inclusion on the sound track itself. *Singles* may not represent the down-the-line grunge aesthetic, but it *does* represent the eclecticism of the grunge header. These bands sound logical together because they don't sound at all logical together. There's a reason they also called this college rock, as you needed a Ph.D. to really deconstruct this stuff. Could Cameron Crowe have known how important his sound track would be? Judging from *Vanilla Sky*, not likely.

ALICE IN CHAINS, *Jar of Flies* (Columbia, 1994): In the wake of the brutal sonic assault that was the heroin-heavy album *Dirt*, Alice in Chains reportedly wrote and recorded this entire EP in a week. When it was released, it shot straight to number one on the Billboard charts, making it the first EP to ever debut at that position. As has been made clear, a lot of grunge bands embraced a certain amount of dichotomy, allowing them to be more than one thing at a time. *Jar of Flies* absolutely lives at both ends of the same spectrum—it doesn't sound like Alice in Chains (or even like grunge), and yet it is the album that defines them (and will define them over time).

Jar of Flies is a largely acoustic-based album (though some people do incorrectly identify it as an "unplugged" album—there are plenty of electric guitars on the album, most notably on "Nutshell"). The songs are quiet meditations that still manage to rock. It's all in the intensity of the delivery—it's clear that Alice in Chains really *loved* these songs. But they're not ballads by any stretch of the imagination. While they do tend to slow things down and soften things up, they still sound like they are delivered from the edge of sanity. In short, you'd have a hard time slow dancing to these songs, which often take turns into minor keys that throw everything into a sort of controlled chaos. This is clearest on "I Stay Away," a song that begins as an airy ballad but then shifts into an off-kilter, doomsday-foretelling riff before the strings and horns show up. For a band whose previous albums were as raw and as base as grunge albums got this side of Mudhoney, it was an incredible and jarring reversal for the band.

One thing that *Jar of Flies* does very well is highlight the stunning voice of Layne Staley, who began his unfortunate downward spiral shortly after *Jar of Flies* was completed (the band never really toured again, and they only released one more original album, a disappointing self-titled record released in 1995). Staley definitely peaked on *Jar of Flies*, as his voice shifted from the psychotic wail he had used on *Facelift* and *Dirt* to an otherworldly moan that was filled with sadness, anger, self-loathing, and regret. His layered vocal lines on "Rotten Apple" and his harmonizing with Cantrell on "No Excuses" are some of the downright *prettiest* sounds made on any rock album in the nineties, grunge or otherwise.

Obviously, as the album is only seven tracks long (and one of those is an instrumental), it's easier to get it right when you don't have as many chances to fail. Also, album closer "Swing on This" still sounds out of place, as though it was written as an afterthought or written separately from the rest of the album. Even so, "No Excuses" will likely be the lasting legacy from *Jar of Flies* and possibly for Alice in Chains as a band. This is extremely bizarre, because the band never made anything else that sounded remotely like "No Excuses" (except for when they tried to rip themselves off on their own self-titled album with a song called "Over Now"). The rolling, lighthearted drums, the singsongy verses, the pretty harmonies, the bubbly bass sound—all of that sounds only vaguely like the band that also produced "Rooster." But that's one of the beautiful things about the grunge era (and this happened *all the time*): In what other time in pop music history could you be remembered for something you're not and still have it be pretty good?

PEARL JAM, *Vs.* (Epic, 1992): If Eddie Vedder was really smart, he would have broken up Pearl Jam right after the release of

Vs., stepping away from the spotlight and retreating to a beach to become the world's richest and most esoteric surfer for the rest of his life. Had Pearl Jam exited on top, they would have been the goddamn Beatles—everybody would *still* be speculating about what their third album would have sounded like and whether or not Crazy Eddie would ever get the band back together. It would have been a genius move (and it likely would have saved us the horrors of *Binaural*).

That's how unbelievably epically fucking huge *Vs.* was in 1992. Still riding the overwhelming crest of success the band received from its debut (and even more notably for the video for "Jeremy"), Pearl Jam did the incredible—they dropped an album at the exact moment when not only were they close to the peak of their fame but also grunge was reaching critical mass (the release of *Vs.* got Vedder on the cover of *Time*). *Vs.* was more than just an album—in 1992, it was validation that rock music could simultaneously exist outside the mainstream and absolutely conquer that same mainstream. The lead-up to the album was huge, and it sold nearly a million copies in its first week of release, an absolutely unheard-of number that broke a record that stood for eight years.

The amazing thing about *Vs.* is that despite its hype, its actually a compelling, difficult album that adhered to Pearl Jam's established sound while throwing in a handful of elements that had to have weirded people out. It opens with a manic, stuttering track called "Go" that no song on *Ten* could have anticipated. It's played with the reckless abandon of a garage band and owes a debt to some punk influences that had yet to appear in Pearl Jam's music. "Go" is followed by another scorching rocker in "Animal" before the band turns to the moody, wistful "Daughter," which saw Vedder deliver one of the gentlest vocal lines he had yet recorded (until he tops himself on side 2 with "Elderly Woman Behind the Counter in a Small Town").

Vs. managed to foreshadow the rest of Pearl Jam's career, as the album's strongest tracks are its ballads, though the molten late-album rockers "Rearviewmirror" and "Leash" are pretty useful. *Vs.* also gave rock fans the first real taste of Pearl Jam's strangeness, as "W.M.A." is an extremely odd, atmospheric, hollow-sounding experiment that laid the groundwork for later sonic adventures such as "Stupid Mop," and "Rats" is a funked-up workout in the tradition of *Ten* b-side "Dirty Frank."

Pearl Jam didn't release any official singles for *Vs.* and never made any videos, yet the album still eventually sold 7 million copies. Though it didn't match the sales power of *Ten*, it was still a phenomenon, and for a brief time it made the rock universe forget about Kurt Cobain and his little band. Vedder and company had lightning in a bottle with *Vs.*, and though it sounds a little bit dated when heard today, it still retains its necessity, if only because it's amazing to think about an album that sounded like this topping the charts and breaking sales records. When history looks back on grunge, Vedder will always be the bridesmaid, but for *Vs.* he was king of the world.

NIRVANA, *Nevermind* (DGC, 1991): So much has been written about *Nevermind* since well before it was released, it's almost impossible to think about it simply as an album of twelve rock songs (plus one hidden track). But the bottom line is that no matter what becomes of any of the other grunge bands over time, no album will ever be as absolutely indispensable as Nirvana's sophomore release. Even without the surrounding story, it would still be an incredible album of kick-ass protopunk; with its story, it's become a legendary icon in rock history, ranking up there with anything the Beatles or Dylan or the Stones ever put out. In fact, if context was considered when ranking the most vital rock albums of all time, a very convincing case could be made for calling *Nevermind* number one, more vital than *Meet the Beatles* or *Exile on Main Street* or *Blonde on Blonde*. It meant that much, not only to rock fans and those in the grunge community but also to the universe at large. Without hyperbole, *Nevermind* changed the course of history.

Sonically speaking, it's weird to even discuss *Nevermind* as a grunge album. If you asked somebody to describe grunge to you, they would probably talk about a band that sounded more like Soundgarden or Mudhoney. But whenever you mention the word "grunge" to somebody, the first band they think of, whether they like it or not, is Nirvana, and they usually think of that picture of the naked baby in the pool right after that. Kurt Cobain often complained that *Nevermind* was overproduced and "too slick," and he's right—it's by far the cleanest-sounding punk album of all time. But the immaculate production quality aids *Nevermind* immensely, as it really highlights the band's secret weapon in the mix: Dave Grohl. Nirvana would still be a great band even if they had Meg White drumming for them, but the fact that Grohl makes his skins sound like Godzilla stomping Tokyo really gives the songs on *Nevermind* the size and the edge that they need. Just think about "Smells Like Teen Spirit" for a second. Everybody knows that opening jangly guitar riff, but when does the song really explode? When Grohl's drum fill comes in and drags the bass along with it. The second Grohl hit that snare the first time, eighties metal was officially dead and grunge, for better or for worse, would change the rock landscape forever.

"Smells Like Teen Spirit" is one of the all-time great album openers, perhaps one of the greatest rock songs ever written, despite the fact that it has one of the goofiest lyric sheets in the history of man. It certainly seemed like Cobain was getting at *something*, but what exactly is less dangerous when the lights are out? And what about that "A mulatto" line? But it was his delivery that absolutely sold it, because even though nobody knew what Cobain was talking about, what they did know was that this guy felt passionate about it. It wasn't just anger, either, as Cobain's voice on *Nevermind* sounds equal parts angry, morose, jaded, and optimistic. Again, Butch Vig's too-slick big rock production helped, as it threw Cobain's voice way up in the mix and brought out all of the subtleties he was capable of (though Steve Albini's capturing of Cobain's vocals on *In Utero* is technically a more accurate representation of Kurt's voice, and it's more impressive as well).

Nirvana proved itself to be a very dynamic group on *Nevermind*, as they could work with atmosphere ("Come as You Are"), unbridled noise ("Territorial Pissings"), mournful ballads ("Something in the Way"), and combinations of all three ("Drain You"). In fact, there are a lot more variations on *Nevermind* than on any other Nirvana release, especially the interesting but somewhat monochromatic *In Utero*. Again, Vig's overproduction, which Cobain viewed as dishonest, probably saved the day.

But ultimately *Nevermind* won't be remembered as an album and not even as a cultural phenomenon but as a representation of what it was like to be young and restless in the nineties. In fact, *Nevermind* has taken on a number of roles in several archetypal tales: It's what happens when a young band is so good the mainstream comes to them; it's what happens when you have too much success too fast; it's what happens when you believe in yourself; it's what happens when you become too committed. When Kurt died, *Nevermind* became an example of the burden of genius. Today it acts as all of those things. Pearl Jam ultimately ended up being the more popular band simply because they stayed together and Soundgarden might represent the grunge sound better, but Nirvana stands alone as the icons of grunge. Fans might not like it, musicians might not like it, and Kurt himself might not have liked it, but it's the truth, and honestly, things could have ended up a lot worse, you know?

—

ACKNOWLEDGMENTS

FIRST AND FOREMOST, I NEED TO THANK MY PARENTS, LARRY AND Susan Anderson, for having me and then never giving up on me, even when I thought being a musical theater actor was a good idea and then when I decided being a rock journalist was a good idea.

Thanks to my agents, Jim Fitzgerald and Anne Garrett, who took an idea that wasn't there and somehow sold it many, many times over.

Thanks to Becki Heller, Rose Hilliard, and everybody at St. Martin's who turned my inane ramblings into an actual book, and for that they deserve a medal.

Thanks to Ryan Anderson for telling the greatest stories I've ever heard and always having a drink at the ready.

Thanks to Nicole Baer for moral support, snuggle time, the occasional meal, and not stabbing me whenever I wax retarded about professional wrestling.

Special thanks to Sean Ryan, one of the few living human beings who has never, ever let me down. I would happily donate my organs to him, even if he didn't need them. In fact, *especially* if he didn't need them.

Throughout the creation of this book, I ranted, I complained, and I talked out my lame theories to a number of different people who were no doubt bored to tears and will probably never speak to me again. I cannot thank these people enough, and they include Sia Michel, Jeanann Pannasch, Caryn Ganz, Phoebe Reilly, Melissa Maerz, Chuck Klosterman, Lane Brown, Jon Dolan, Catherine Davis, Doug Brod, Charles Aaron, Dave Itzkoff, Peter Gaston, Marc Spitz, Kathy Kemp, Bethany Mezick, Jennifer Santana, Damian DeMartino, Liz Macfarlane, Devin Pedzwater, Kory Kennedy, Kaitlin Fontana, Katie Heath, Illyria Turk, Alison Goran, Cat Oppenheimer, Tricia Summers, Emily Tan, Arielle Castillo, Morgan Clendaniel, Jennifer Clay, Ashley Bryan, Lisa Tauber, Jenna Payne, Nicola Crockett, Lauren Beck, Katy Lindenmuth, Adam Raymond, Molly Wardlaw, Marti Zimlin, Paul Familetti, Maria Raha, Laura Sinagra, Chris Ryan, Ryan Dombal, Sean Howe, Annabel Bentley, Tim Purtell, Jake Thomas, Dave Sticher, Jacob Brown, Katja Andreiev, Sam Bourne, Mike Newman, Amanda Peck, Fred Nicolaus, Quentin Little, Krystyna Nicholls, Scott Gramling, Adam Winer, Sam Barclay, Phillip Crandall, Tom Conlon, Meg Conaton, Jake Bronstein, Anthony Bozza, Jim and Noreen Ryan, Nora and Al Taylor, Mike Holzman, Jennifer Maerz, Steve Manning, Nils Bernstein, Mark Arm, John Roderick, Ever Kipp, Andrew Pinnow, the Albert family, the Zirolli family, Lauren Graczyk, Sarah Curran, Sarah Moore, Sara Howe, Kira Lauren, Libby Weintraub, Erin Monju, Emma Bedard, and that waitress with the fantastic ankles at Zeek's Pizza in Seattle.

I would also like to thank the following fictional characters, inanimate objects, people I have never met, and general sources of good in the universe: Horace the Penguin, Awful Man, Mister Softee, Mr. Met, my iBook G4, Kurt Angle, Professor Top, Ms. Pac-Man, Scooby-Doo, deadspin.com, half.com, hlcomic.com, Jordan Capri,

Coked-Up Nemo, Werner Herzog, Olmec, Batzarro, *Astonishing X-Men*, and Theresa Heinz Kerry.

Special thanks to Robert and Lilian Anderson, Jeff and Lynn Dwyer, and Leonard and Connie Anderson for their indestructible wills and their unending support of my silly little career.

This book was fueled by Chipotle burritos, Jamba Juice's Coldbuster, Gatorade Rain, Boylan's ginger ale, Glenlivet, Samuel Adams, the chili at Old Town Bar, and the Bluegrass and Booze Brunch at Nolita House.